HISTORICAL SKETCHES

Portrait of Mary Baker Eddy

HISTORICAL SKETCHES

FROM THE LIFE OF MARY BAKER EDDY AND THE HISTORY OF CHRISTIAN SCIENCE

CLIFFORD P. SMITH

THE CHRISTIAN SCIENCE PUBLISHING SOCIETY
BOSTON, MASSACHUSETTS, U.S.A.

PUBLISHER'S NOTE

Changes made in this edition were recommended by the Archives of The Mother Church and are based on material pertaining to the life of Mary Baker Eddy which was not available when the author wrote his manuscript.

Library of Congress Catalog Card No. 42-13439
ISBN 0-87510-005-8

Printed in the United States of America

FOREWORD

This small book is designed to be biographical as well as historical. Its chapters were first published in The Christian Science Journal *as a series of Historical and Biographical Papers. The change of title has been made for convenience in printing.*

These Historical Sketches, united by their connection with Christian Science and Mary Baker Eddy, are intended to furnish facts and information of a dependable nature. Especially, this is a book intended to furnish a factual basis for just conclusions by fair-minded readers in regard to Mrs. Eddy and the beneficent results which have ensued from her discovery and work. The author's positions in the service of The Mother Church have given him ample opportunities to be correctly informed as to these subjects.

CLIFFORD P. SMITH, *Editor*

Bureau of History and Records
The First Church of Christ, Scientist
Boston, Massachusetts

March, 1941

CONTENTS

Contents

PART THREE — HISTORY

ILLUSTRATIONS

PART ONE

BIOGRAPHY

CHAPTER I

New Hampshire as It Was

NEW HAMPSHIRE, the New England state in which Mary Baker Eddy, the Discoverer and Founder of Christian Science, was born and educated, is of more than passing interest to students of Christian Science. A hundred years ago, the southern part of New Hampshire was a farming region dotted here and there by villages and towns. There were small factories and mills in most of the towns. The Merrimack River, flowing from the north through the middle of the southern part of the state, until it turned eastward toward the Atlantic Ocean at the border of Massachusetts, carried freight by boats from and to places along the river. A canal from where the river turned eastward connected it with Boston. Other canals and locks along the river, around falls and rapids, enabled boats to go from Boston to Concord. Most of the canal boats were drawn by horses or pushed with poles.

At that time, there were no railroads in New Hampshire. When things could not be delivered by boats, they were hauled in wagons or sleds drawn by horses or oxen. The mails were carried and people traveled on horses, in

[1]

buggies, carriages, or sleighs, or in stagecoaches. People went to places then by walking much more than is common now. Some of them would walk five miles or farther to church every Sunday. There were stages that made regular trips between the larger towns. The fastest stages, drawn by four horses, could go about eight miles an hour on the best roads. The best roads were called turnpikes, and people had to pay for using them, but even they were poor as compared with the best roads of today.

Until after 1835, New Hampshire houses were heated by fireplaces or stoves. Furnaces were not in common use. Houses were lighted by candles. Kerosene lamps and gaslight were later products. So were friction matches. There were newspapers for New Hampshire readers in 1835, Boston papers as well as local papers, but news traveled slowly, no faster than it would be told by one person to another or carried by mail. The telegraph began to be used in 1844, and telegraph lines had to be constructed after that. People read newspapers, magazines and books, and read them carefully, especially the Bible.

In the 1830's, peddlers were a customary part of country life. They visited farmhouses regularly, and sold articles of any kind that could be carried in a pack or on horseback. Incidentally, a peddler carried news and was likely to have as many acquaintances as a village postmaster. One item of a letter written in 1844 by Abigail

Ambrose Baker to her daughter Mary, after the latter married Major Glover, was this: "Your pocket handkerchief peddler called."

In another letter at this time, Mrs. Baker gave Mrs. Glover the following picture of the Baker home during an evening: "Martha is much engaged in sewing but cannot lay out her work to good advantage, having *new patterns*. We wish you were here to assist her. . . . Dear Mahala sits braiding, your father sits reading, you know I am always at work. We miss your good cheer." Martha was Mary's next older sister; Mahala was Mahala Sanborn, the family's house servant.

In 1840, the larger New Hampshire towns were Portsmouth, Dover, Nashua, and Concord. In this list, the largest town is named first. At this time, Concord had about five thousand inhabitants, and it had an importance, as the capital of the state, beyond its size. Concord also had the advantage of being on the Merrimack River, and of being the farthest point up the river to which the canal boats could go. There were two bridges across the river there. Concord was the beginning or end for a number of lines of stagecoaches. Then, too, the famous Concord stagecoach, a particular kind of vehicle, was made there. Concord was noted for the number and quality of its taverns. It also had a number of societies, agricultural, musical, Bible, and missionary, besides four or five bookstores, at least three newspapers and a literary journal. One of the Concord newspapers, *New Hampshire Patriot,* had a circulation that extended into all parts of the state.

Bow, the birthplace of Mary Baker Eddy, was an area of farms, a rural township. It was a town in the New England sense of this term, adjoining Concord. The northeast boundary of Bow was the Merrimack River, which had a twenty-five-foot falls here that was passed by a canal on the Bow side. In 1840, Bow had a meeting house, ten district schools, fifteen mills of different kinds, and about a thousand inhabitants. Many of them attended church and did their shopping in Concord.

Eighteen miles north of Concord was Sanbornton Bridge on the Winnepesaukee River. It is now named Tilton. In 1840, this town had 2745 people, and had its own advantages. Among them were falls or rapids in the river, which furnished power for factories or mills, good schools, and the Sanbornton Academy, which had well-known teachers and was open to both boys and girls. At that time, not every town of two thousand five hundred or three thousand inhabitants had a newspaper, but Sanbornton Bridge had one; it also had a publisher of books. Besides three churches, it had a Society for the Reformation of Morals. The larger churches in Concord and in Sanbornton Bridge had educated ministers.

A few miles west of Sanbornton Bridge was another town, named Franklin, on the Merrimack River. North of Franklin and Sanbornton Bridge was Plymouth, where

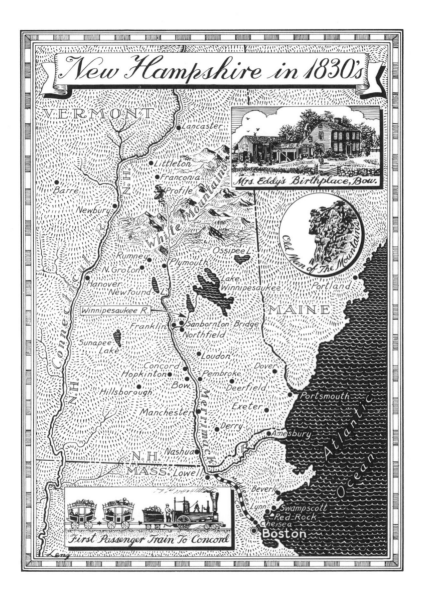

New Hampshire in 1830's

Mrs. Eddy's Birthplace, Bow.

Old Man of The Mountains

First Passenger Train To Concord

there was another academy. Still farther north were the beautiful and rugged White Mountains, which attracted tourists and visitors then as they do now. Plymouth, Sanbornton Bridge, and Concord were on a main highway that connected the northern part of New Hampshire with the southern part and with the adjacent parts of Massachusetts, including Lynn and Boston.

Concord is about seventy-five miles north of Boston, which was and is much the most important city in the group of six states called New England. In 1840, Boston had ninety-three thousand inhabitants. The first railroad built north from Boston was completed to Lowell in 1835, to Nashua in 1840, and to Concord in 1842.[1] Of course, it was crude as compared with a modern railroad. On it, however, a passenger could travel from Boston to Concord in less than half a day; and one could do this with some degree of comfort at any time of year. What is more important, a short railroad train could carry many times as much freight as could be hauled by a long line of wagons, and a railroad could carry freight much faster than it would be conveyed by either boats or wagons.

In his book *Division and Reunion, 1829–1889,* the historian and statesman Woodrow Wilson speaks of the year 1829 as the beginning of a new epoch in American history. He explains: "The new nation was now in the first flush of assured success. . . . It had once more proved

---

[1] *History of New Hampshire,* by John N. McClintock, p. 563.

the capacity of the English race to combine the rude strength and bold initiative that can subdue a wilderness with those self-controlling habits of ordered government that can build free and permanent states." Speaking of education at that time, the same author says: "New Englanders of all sorts and conditions had been affected by a system of popular education, although they had by no means all partaken of it. . . . Books as well as life, old knowledge as well as new experience, schools as well as struggles with Nature, had gone to make up the Americans of the time."

In New England, the decades from 1830 to 1850 were notable as an era of betterments in the conditions of human life. "Democracy was coming into its own, and expressing itself rather in terms of the brotherhood of human beings than in those of abstract equality in political rights and obligations."[1] Among the causes or movements that attracted attention during this period were the betterment of prisons, doing away with imprisonment for debt, shortening the hours of labor, promotion of temperance, abolition of slavery, avoidance of war, liberality or tolerance in religion, improvement of public schools, and getting for women the right to speak in public.

A hundred years ago, the boys and girls of New Hampshire had access to better schools than were likely to be found in more than a few other regions. In this state,

---

[1] *New England in the Republic, 1776–1850,* by James Truslow Adams, p. 367.

there were common schools everywhere, and most of them had fair teachers. Higher education was provided by a college, by academies or high schools, and by tutors, most of whom were educated ministers. Dartmouth College, at Hanover, one of the best-known colleges in New England, was founded in 1769. Phillips Academy, at Exeter, the best known of the New Hampshire academies, was founded in 1781. These academies were like high schools in the scope of their studies, but were likely to have superior teachers. The academies were conducted by private owners, who charged a fee or tuition for each pupil. Some of the academies admitted only boys or only girls; others were open to all who had enough preparation for the subjects to be studied.

New Hampshire a century ago was very religious. The people retained the piety and zeal of their ancestors who left England for New England mainly for religious reasons. New England was settled by Englishmen who wished to live in strict accord with their religious views, who had not been allowed to do this in England, and who expected to have more freedom in the New World, where they could regulate their own lives. Afterwards, people moved from one colony to another, as from Massachusetts to New Hampshire, because they sought more religious freedom than had been allowed to them where they were. So, New Hampshire people of a century ago were ardent Christians; they had a keen interest in the Christian religion as they construed it; and they were zealous, not only for themselves and their children, but also for their friends and neighbors.

Speaking of New Englanders in 1790, a professor of history has attributed to them "the four gospels of education, thrift, ingenuity, and righteousness."[1] As applied to New Hampshire, this remark could have been extended to a later time. Nearly all the people who lived in New Hampshire in the 1830's were born there or in adjacent states. Comparatively few of the many immigrants from Ireland and elsewhere who arrived in New England from 1830 to 1840 entered New Hampshire. Nearly all of them settled in Massachusetts cities or in seaboard towns.

An English author, Adam Hodgson, who visited the United States in the 1820's put his observations into a book, *Letters from North America*, commended as a particularly well-balanced account of America. He was delighted with the people in New England. "There I see on every side a hardy, robust, industrious, enterprising population; better fed, better clothed, better educated than I ever saw before; and more intelligent and at least as moral as the corresponding classes of our own countrymen."[2]

Other characteristics of the people of New England or of New Hampshire have been noted and emphasized

---

[1] *Oxford History of the United States,* by S. E. Morison, Vol. I, p. 12.
[2] *American Social History as Recorded by British Travelers,* compiled by Allan Nevins, p. 26.

by other writers. In his report for 1847, the New Hampshire Commissioner of Education said, "It seems to be the destiny of New England, and eminently so of New Hampshire, to produce mind."[1] This assertion appears complacent; yet, it extended to the future, and, in proportion to her population, New Hampshire had already given birth to an extraordinary number of persons, besides Mrs. Eddy, who were distinguished for their intelligence. Of them an impressive list could be made. Of her it can be said that she is steadily becoming recognized by correctly informed persons everywhere as one of the most illustrious of all women—as one of the greatest of all humane and spiritual thinkers.

---

[1] *New England in the Republic, 1776–1850*, by James Truslow Adams, p. 363.

CHAPTER II

Mrs. Eddy's Parents

"AMONG the earliest of the New England settlers, the Bakers and Ambroses were pioneer families of marked distinction, as the almost forgotten local histories of Massachusetts and New Hampshire attest in many ways."[1] Mrs. Eddy's parents were from these families.

They differed from each other in individual ways, and both of them had more culture and more varied interests than were common in their day among men and women of equal prosperity. Yet, Mark Baker and Abigail Ambrose Baker can be described as typical New Hampshire people of their time. They were intelligent, thrifty, religious, and they were independent thinkers. Further, they were charitable, hospitable, and public-spirited.

From their marriage in 1807 to 1836, Mr. and Mrs. Baker lived on their farm in the town of Bow. From 1836 to 1849, they lived on a farm one mile from Sanbornton Bridge which they acquired instead of the one in Bow. In 1849, Mark Baker moved into Sanbornton Bridge. While

---

[1] *The Ancestry of Mary Baker Eddy,* by William Montgomery Clemens, p. 10.

[10]

the Bakers lived in Bow, they did most of their buying and selling in Concord, which was the nearest center of business and population. Afterward, their business center was Sanbornton Bridge.

At his different places of residence, Mark Baker held the following offices or positions: agent of the town of Bow in regard to caring for the poor; clerk of the Congregational church of Bow; delegate of his church to church conferences; coroner for the County of Rockingham; justice of the peace for the County of Belknap; Sunday School superintendent for the Congregational church at Sanbornton Bridge; trustee of Sanbornton Academy; quartermaster sergeant of a regiment in the New Hampshire militia; sergeant major of the same regiment; and sometimes acting chaplain thereof.

In the first of these offices, Mark Baker had an exceptional experience. He argued a dispute and got a decision for the town of Bow against the town of Loudon when the latter was represented by Franklin Pierce, then a prominent lawyer and politician, who later became President of the United States.

Mark Baker was a fairly well-known man in a number of communities, particularly in Bow, Concord, Pembroke, Hillsborough, Sanbornton Bridge, and Northfield. He was devoted to the Congregational church, but had acquaintances among the ministers of other denominations, and was fond of debating doctrinal points with them. Ministers often enjoyed his hospitality, partly for the purpose of engaging in discussions with him. Morning and evening devotions, Bible reading and prayer, were part of his daily routine. He asked a blessing and gave thanks before and after every meal. He kept the Sabbath rigidly. He was also strict in regard to decorum and propriety. Thus, in 1836, when his daughters Abigail and Martha were invited to a dancing school at Sanbornton Bridge he would not allow them to accept.

Mark and Abigail Ambrose Baker were members of a church in Bow from 1809 to 1829. At first, it was called the Union Church of Christ in Bow. In 1822, its name was changed to the Congregational Church in Bow. After it was dissolved in 1829, they became attendants at churches in Pembroke and Concord until 1831. Then, they became members of First Congregational Church of Concord, one of the best-known churches in New Hampshire. In 1838, after they moved to near Sanbornton Bridge, they joined the Congregational church there.

At all times, the Baker family, not always including the boys, attended church meetings regularly. In Concord, on Sundays, they usually attended morning and afternoon services. Between the services, the older members of the family, as well as the younger, enjoyed social contacts, but the boys and girls were expected to observe the Sabbath in the old-time New England way.

Mark Baker was an affectionate husband and intended

The "Old North" Church in Concord, New Hampshire

to be an affectionate father. As his children approached adult years, they sometimes believed that he was not so considerate of them as he could and should have been. The boys found their own occupations helped but little by him. The daughters sometimes had to insist on what they regarded as their dues or rights. For instance, when the family moved to the farm near Sanbornton Bridge he sold his carriage with other items of property, and did not buy a new one until the eldest daughter, Abigail, who was then twenty, declared that she would never again go anywhere in a wagon.

At different times, all of the six children had disagreements with their father, Mrs. Baker always exerting her influence for harmony and mutual understanding. In some respects, he appeared to be more frugal than circumstances required. In other respects, he was generous. He was especially so in cases of misfortune or need. In one instance, he allowed an invalid widow and her daughter to occupy a cottage free of rent.

Mark Baker was said to be a very determined man who never changed his mind. A more accurate statement would be that he was a positive man who formed individual opinions and acted on them. Thus, he voted with the party of Thomas Jefferson, James Madison, and James Monroe from 1808 to 1828; then he joined other followers of Andrew Jackson in forming a new party. Later, when slavery became an acute issue between northern and southern states in counsel, at all times cheerful and hopeful, she was the presiding genius of a lovely circle and a happy home."

Her letters that have survived to the present time are those of a loving mother and an educated woman. At times, she disclosed a philosophic vein. Thus, in a letter of April 9, 1844, to her daughter Mary, she wrote, "Forget the past, enjoy the present, hope for the future." So, also, in a letter dated September 2, 1848, owned by the Longyear Foundation, Mrs. Baker wrote to her son George: "I have been reading Tappan on the Will. That is excellent." Doubtless, she referred to *The Doctrine of the Will applied to Moral Agency and Responsibility* (1841) by Henry Philip Tappan, who had been professor of Moral and Intellectual Philosophy in New York University and was to be the first president of the University of Michigan.

Except for comparatively short times, Mrs. Eddy lived with her parents until 1849, when she was twenty-eight years old. Then, her mother having passed on, she lived with her father for another year, when he remarried. Thereafter (until his death in 1865) Mrs. Eddy never again lived in her father's home.

Of all the persons with whom Mary Baker Eddy came in contact, her mother must have affected her much the most. She loved her mother devotedly, and they were together most of the time during the years which included the most impressionable part of the daughter's life.

CHAPTER III

ONE OF MRS. EDDY'S BROTHERS

ANOTHER lasting influence during twenty years of the same formative period was that of Mrs. Eddy's brother, Albert Baker.

Born on February 5, 1810, he was eleven years older than she. Among all her relations, including father, mother, three brothers, two sisters, and more distant relatives, her mother and he, throughout her childhood and girlhood, were closest to her in companionship and in thought. He passed on at the early age of thirty-one, after having entered upon a legal and political career of exceptional promise.

As a child and boy, Albert Baker lived on his parents' farm at Bow. After attending the common school near his home and Pembroke Academy, he entered Dartmouth College at Hanover, New Hampshire, in 1830. To pay the cost of a college education, he taught school and did tutoring. For one period he was principal of the Hillsborough Academy.

For *The Bench and Bar of New Hampshire*, published in 1914, Charles Henry Bell, also an alumnus of Pembroke Academy and of Dartmouth College, and afterwards

Governor of New Hampshire, contributed a sketch of Albert Baker containing the following statements (p. 161): "In college he was an excellent scholar, and persistent to the extent of sometimes defending his own opinions in the recitation room against the doctrines of the professors. As a lawyer he was well-read, sharp in making points, and unyielding in maintaining them. . . . Though he died in early manhood, he had already made his mark in law and in politics. . . . Young as he was, he was an acknowledged party leader at the time of his decease."

In Dartmouth College, Albert Baker was a member of the United Fraternity from his freshman year. He also became its vice-president and its president in his junior and senior years. The objects of the United Fraternity were "literary and forensic improvement." Before graduating, he was also elected to Phi Beta Kappa. As part of the exercises on commencement day, he delivered the salutatory address. He graduated in 1834, receiving the degree A. B. He also graduated "with the reputation of being one of the finest students who had ever attended that institution." [1]

In 1834, an A. B. degree from Dartmouth College required work in the following departments: classical, mathematical, physical, rhetorical, besides intellectual and moral philosophy. Instead of ending early in June, the college year extended to the latter part of August. Surely,

---

[1] Browne's *History of Hillsborough*, Vol. I, p. 414.

Albert Baker was able to tutor Mary Baker, his physically frail sister, as she has said. [1]

After graduating from Dartmouth College, Albert Baker studied law for nearly three years and then began to practice this profession. For about two years, he studied at Hillsborough, New Hampshire, with the Hon. Franklin Pierce, afterward President of the United States. He then studied in Boston with the Hon. Richard Fletcher, later a justice of the Supreme Judicial Court of Massachusetts. At that time, Hillsborough, twenty-seven miles from Concord, was a comparatively important town. There, in 1837, Albert Baker began his legal practice as successor to the Hon. Franklin Pierce.

Albert Baker's father and Franklin Pierce's father, Benjamin Pierce, who was Governor of New Hampshire from 1827 to 1829, were personal friends. Both the Pierces became interested in Albert Baker because of this fact, because of his creditable record at Dartmouth, and because he appeared to be a youth of exceptional promise. In appearance, he was said to resemble Andrew Jackson. The Pierces are mentioned in Mrs. Eddy's writings. [2]

In the following quotation, "the general" is Benjamin Pierce, and "the homestead" is the Pierce homestead at Hillsborough.

---

[1] See *Retrospection and Introspection*, p. 10; *Miscellany*, p. 310.
[2] See *Retrospection and Introspection*, p. 6; *Miscellany*, pp. 308, 309.

"Albert Baker was the son of Mark Baker, an old friend of the general's, and while he was at Dartmouth the Pierces had become interested in the boy and had helped him. They invited him, when he graduated in 1834, to live at the homestead and study law with Franklin, the general paying his expenses during his novitiate. This association had rather far-reaching influence; the polish and learning of Franklin Pierce and his protégé, Albert Baker, so impressed the latter's little sister that she too became anxious for the advantages of an education. Later, when she had become Mrs. Mary Baker Eddy and had successfully founded The First Church of Christ, Scientist, she attributed her initial intellectual stimulus to the example and tutoring of her brother during his vacations from Dartmouth and his visits home from Hillsborough."[1]

A letter from Albert Baker written when he was studying law in Boston indicates that he paid his expenses there by selling his classical books and by borrowing money. The fact that Mary Baker had intellectual impulses of her own in her early years is to be inferred from a letter from him to her dated Hillsborough, March 27, 1837. In this letter, "Abi" was their sister Abigail. Solomon Wilson was an instructor in the Sanbornton Academy.

My dear Sister,

I have an opportunity of sending a letter by a friend of mine, Mr. Harrison Andrews, who is going to Sanbornton with the

---

[1] *Biography of Franklin Pierce*, by Roy Franklin Nichols, 1931, pp. 80–81.

intention of attending the academy. I take great pleasure in introducing him to your acquaintance. You will find him a sterling fellow, a little enthusiastick, but none of Sol Wilson about him. What is that poor devil doing? I hope you treat him as he deserves, with entire neglect. Abi will recollect Andrews' sister, a particular friend of hers. He is a very close student, and is as much given to *discursive talking* as yourself, though he has not quite so much poetry at his command. . . .

Your affect. br.

A. Baker

Incidentally, the foregoing quotation illustrates the closeness of the relation between this older brother, twenty-seven, and younger sister, nearly sixteen.

Albert Baker gave friendly advice, not only to his youngest sister Mary, but to his younger brother George. The following instance from a letter dated November 23, 1837, is one of several: "My rule is *to do the best I can*, and whatever happens, if it cannot be avoided, to submit cheerfully. Is not this true philosophy? Now apply this rule. Have you done all you could do? If so, be content with the event; if not, learn by the past how to regulate the future."

Albert Baker's letters to his brother George included the following references to their sister Mary:

August 24, 1836. "Mary has attended school all summer, and is quite as well as could be expected."

October 16, 1837. "I received a letter from Martha yesterday. Her health is improving and so is Mary's. When

I came to Hillsborough, I never expected to see her again. Martha tells me she commenced going to school at your expense but was obliged to abandon it." The Martha mentioned in the foregoing letter was another sister. Presumably the school which called for the payment of expense was an academy, and Mary Baker is known to have attended the Sanbornton Academy at Sanbornton Bridge. The latter must have been the one mentioned in Albert's letter dated March 27, 1837, for the Bakers lived then near Sanbornton Bridge.

Before he decided to settle at Hillsborough, Albert Baker almost yielded to the attractions of the great and promising West. In particular, he gave much thought to Burlington, where one of his friends in Dartmouth College had gone. In 1837, Burlington was a booming town in the Iowa district of Wisconsin Territory, and was about to become the capital of the Territory of Iowa, constituted by an Act of Congress in 1838. This friend, James W. Grimes, afterward Governor of Iowa and United States Senator from Iowa, presented the advantages of the West in most attractive terms. But Franklin Pierce was moving to Concord and was to be much in Washington as a senator from New Hampshire; hence, he induced Baker to settle at Hillsborough so that he could attend to Pierce's unfinished business and care for his aged parents, to whom Baker was already obligated.

Although admitted to practice law in Massachusetts

as well as New Hampshire, Albert Baker appears to have practiced only in New Hampshire. His career as a lawyer can be traced by the letters and papers that he left when he passed on. Kept by his brother George, who administered his estate, they were preserved by George's son, and purchased at last by the Longyear Foundation. Among these papers is a closely written book of notes which proves that Albert Baker was careful, discriminating, and methodical as a law student. Twenty-five letters from Franklin Pierce, nearly all of them dated from Washington, show that he regarded Baker as a dependable lawyer, capable of attending to important business or litigation. Other letters and papers indicate that landowners along the line of the railroad being constructed northward to Concord turned to him for the protection of their rights, and that he had a considerable number of clients in Boston.

The reports of decisions by the Supreme Court of New Hampshire from 1838 to 1840 contain five cases in which Baker appeared for different parties, a fact that indicates his immediate success as a lawyer. In one of these cases (*Bennett vs. Dutton*, 10 N. H. 481) he acted for a stage line or combination of such lines, the decision determining an obligation of a stage line as a carrier of passengers. At this time, the stage lines were at the height of their prosperity; hence, they were desirable clients.

The newspapers of his time as well as the letters kept by Albert Baker show that he attained quickly a prominent position in politics and public affairs. Senator Pierce's letters to him dealt with both law and politics. The representative in the United States Congress from the Hillsborough district, the Hon. Charles G. Atherton, consulted him as a leading member of their party. Among the letters kept by Baker were two from John C. Calhoun of South Carolina, who had been Vice-President of the United States and continued to be prominent in public life. They corresponded about a dispute between Georgia and Maine concerning the return of slaves to their owners. After having been a delegate to several district and state conventions, and a member of the Democratic State Central Committee, Baker, in 1840, was a delegate to the Democratic National Convention, held at Baltimore, which nominated candidates for President and Vice-President.

Albert Baker was elected to the New Hampshire House of Representatives when he was twenty-nine years old. Annual elections enabled him to serve for three years, 1839, 1840, 1841. The New Hampshire papers of that time, particularly the best of them, the *New Hampshire Patriot and State Gazette*, continually depicted Baker as taking a prominent part in the work of each session. He evinced an active interest in all of the more important legislative subjects, was a frequent speaker on debated questions, and evidently was regarded as one of the two or three most influential representatives. In his branch of the legislature he was a member, during each session, of its most important committee, the judiciary, and during his last term he was the chairman. His legislative work attracted favorable attention throughout New Hampshire and a degree of favorable notice from other states. In all probability, he was about to be promoted to the United States Congress.

Albert Baker became "an exceedingly popular young man in the town and the State." [1] The reasons were many, but especially they were his admirable motives, his disinterested purposes, his intellectual freshness, and his persistence in the pursuit of fairness, justice, and individual rights. For such reasons, he received and accepted more than a few invitations to deliver lectures and orations, at least one of which was delivered in Boston. There, on January 3, 1840, he delivered a lecture on the legitimate objects of legislation for the Bay State Association of Democratic Young Men. Even his lectures, much more his orations and political speeches, always aroused interest and often evoked enthusiasm.

The subjects to which Baker gave particular attention as a member of the New Hampshire legislature included the abolition of imprisonment for debt, the revision of election laws, the protection of graves from molestation, the powers to be conferred on corporations, including railroads, whether a town should be authorized to buy stock in a railroad, when actions could be maintained against

---

[1] Hurd's *History of Hillsborough County*, 1925, p. 409.

[25]

sheriffs, the holding of courts at convenient times, the relations between states in regard to slavery, the prevention of fraud by bankers, and economy in the administration of government.

Baker's health was dubious for several years before he succumbed. Thus on April 28, 1837, just before he began his legal practice, he wrote to his brother George, "I left the hospital at Boston last Thursday. . . . I have done nothing since the first of March." In a letter dated October 16, 1837, he spoke of his health, with one exception, as "unusually good," but later in the same letter used the words "if my health continues." In the same letter he also said, "I attend constantly at my office and love the work." Some of his friends believed that he overworked.

Albert Baker's decease on October 17, 1841, was followed by remarkable tributes. Mrs. Eddy has preserved one of them on page 7 of her *Retrospection and Introspection.* It was from the editor of *Hill's Daily Patriot,* who had been among Baker's political associates but had changed to a contrary position. Other political opponents also spoke in similar terms, notably the editors of the *New Hampshire Statesman,* an organ of the Whig Party.

The following excerpts are part of a letter from "an intimate friend of Mr. Baker," which was printed and reprinted in several newspapers, including the *New Hampshire Patriot and State Gazette* for November 4, 1841:

"Albert Baker was elected to the state legislature in

1839, and has remained a member of that body for three successive years. His public services while in this situation, where he at once assumed a leading and conspicuous rank, are, it is believed, too well known to the people of this state to require comments.

"He went emphatically for the greatest good of the greatest number. He hated tyranny and despised fraud. He was no stickler for expediency. His only question was —What is right? and that which in his idea was the right, he would pursue fearless of consequences. His maxim was that what is right must be politic. . . .

"He had a strong and a disciplined intellect. In manner he was always forcible, often eloquent, and at times his lips seemed touched with a coal from the very altar of truth. . . . And he did not labor without his reward. *He* has gone, but his works remain. His name will live after him. In his short life he lived long and effected much."

Mrs. Eddy often spoke of her brother Albert to members of her household. Only a month or so before she passed on, she spoke of him as the most scientific man that she ever knew before the discovery of Christian Science.

CHAPTER IV

Two of Mrs. Eddy's Kinsmen

ONE of Mrs. Eddy's first cousins was Hildreth H. Smith. Their mothers were sisters. He was born at Deerfield, New Hampshire, on February 17, 1820, one year before she was, and became a distinguished educator and scholar.

After attending common schools and the Foxcroft Academy, Mr. Smith graduated from Bowdoin College, Brunswick, Maine, in 1842, where he made an excellent record. Between terms at Bowdoin, he taught school to help pay his expenses there. From this college, he received the degree A. B. in 1842 and the degree A. M. in 1845.

After graduating from college, Mr. Smith taught school while carrying on advanced academic studies and studying law. Having been admitted to the practice of law, he engaged in this practice at Baltimore, Maryland, but after a few years he returned to educational pursuits.

In 1851, he and another man opened the school at Newton, North Carolina, which soon became Catawba College. He was a professor in this college and its first president. As a professor, his subjects were mathematics, natural science, and modern languages.

[28]

In 1856, Professor Smith was appointed professor of modern languages in the University of North Carolina. During the American Civil War, he added ancient languages and mathematics to his regular work. He continued with this institution until 1868, when it was closed temporarily because of conditions resulting from the war.

After resigning from the University of North Carolina in 1868, Professor Smith opened a school for boys at Lincolnton, North Carolina, which added to his reputation as an educator. In future years, it was considered distinctly creditable for one to have been trained at this school under his supervision.

In 1867 and 1869, the philanthropist George Peabody established a fund called the Peabody Education Fund for the purpose of developing educational facilities in the southern states. His two endowments amounted to more than two million dollars. At different times Professor Smith was connected with the administration of this fund.

In 1872, he moved to Atlanta, Georgia, to fill the first of a series of positions in which he helped to improve public schools in the southern states. These positions included the superintendency of schools in Atlanta and in Shelbyville, Tennessee, and Houston, Texas. In Houston for two years from October of 1877, as general superintendent of public schools, he planned and organized what was said to be the first system of graded schools in Texas. It included common schools and a high school having general, classical, and normal courses. Then from 1879 to 1881, he was president of the State Normal School at Huntsville, Texas, which is now Sam Houston State Teachers College. For these positions, or most of them, he was recommended by representatives of the Peabody Education Fund.

In 1881, Professor Smith received the degree LL. D. from Baylor University, not long before he returned to Atlanta. From 1882 to 1908, he lived in Atlanta, dividing his attention between educational interests and the literary department of the *Atlanta Journal.*

Dr. Smith was a man of exceptionally broad culture. He was versed in mathematics, astronomy, and natural science. He also had an extraordinary knowledge of history and languages. It was said that he could compose the history of any country without consulting a reference work. Besides reading Greek and Latin, he both read and spoke French, German, Italian, and Spanish. He loved poetry, and could read the classics of all periods in their original languages.

As young people of about the same age, Mary Baker and Hildreth Smith were more than cousins; they were also intimate friends. They were frequently together; then, having kindred tastes, they were apt to discuss philosophy and to read or recite poetry, including her own verses. The following statement is one that he made in 1906, when her son and one of her nephews were making trouble for her in the guise of "next friends":

Two of Mrs. Eddy's Kinsmen

"I have known the Rev. Mary Baker Eddy from childhood. She is my first cousin. Her mother was my mother's younger sister. She was always a beloved visitor in our home. We corresponded for several years while I was in college; the correspondence ended with my regret. I have always admired my cousin's sincerity and devotion to good works. Her brother Albert was one of the ablest lawyers of New Hampshire; but Mary was deemed the most scholarly member of her family. She has always held a sacred place in my heart. It gives me great pleasure to find that God is always protecting her."

The following is part of an editorial in the *Atlanta Journal* for September 14, 1908, when Dr. Smith passed on:

"His was a scholarship such as the South has rarely ever seen, combined with a gentleness and courtesy, the fine flavor of a high gentility and a native vigor of intellect which could not fail to place him among the notable figures of the South. To all these has been added length of days, and during eighty-eight years he has exerted the wholesome example of a blameless life. He had the happy faculty not only of acquiring but of imparting information and he readily became one of the most successful educators in the country. More than one generation, developing character and intellect under his discipline and tutelage, rises up to call him blessed."

Another of Mrs. Eddy's kinsmen was Henry M. Baker. His paternal grandfather and her father were brothers. He

[31]

was born at Bow, New Hampshire, on January 11, 1841; hence, he was her junior by twenty years.

After attending the common school near his home, he attended the academies at Pembroke, Hopkinton, and Sanbornton Bridge. From 1859 to 1863, he was in Dartmouth College, graduating with the degree A. B. Three years later, he received from Dartmouth the degree A. M.

In 1866, he graduated from the law school of George Washington University, then called Columbian University, receiving the degree LL. B. Until 1874, he was a clerk in the war and treasury departments of government at Washington, when he resigned his clerkship and entered the practice of law in Washington. In this practice, he was conspicuously successful.

While occupied in Washington, Mr. Baker maintained his legal residence in New Hampshire and his interest in New Hampshire affairs. So, in 1886, he was made judge advocate general of the New Hampshire National Guard and given the rank of brigadier general. Afterwards he was usually spoken of as General Baker. Then, in 1890, he was elected to the New Hampshire senate. In the New Hampshire legislature, he was chairman of the senate's judiciary committee and chairman of a special joint committee to revise and codify the public statutes. As a whole, his legislative work was regarded as an exceptional public service.

By reason of General Baker's record as a state senator,

he was elected in 1892 to the United States House of Representatives. Again elected in 1894, he did not seek re-election in 1896, but resumed the practice of law in Washington. In the National Congress, his long experience in Washington proved to be of great value; he debated convincingly on many subjects; he was also a member of important committees, including agricultural and judiciary. Several of his speeches were printed and circulated widely. While he was in Congress as a Republican the majority was Democratic; hence, he was a prominent figure among the minority.

As stated in the *Biographical Directory of Members of the American Congress:* "Henry M. Baker was always a close student and keen observer. The cultivation of a taste for literature has been for him a pleasure and a recreation." He was also a profound student of history, and accepted many invitations to deliver addresses on historical and literary subjects. Other positions held by General Baker were president of the alumni of Dartmouth College, president of the New Hampshire Society of the Sons of the American Revolution, chairman of Committee on Rules in the New Hampshire Constitutional Convention in 1902, and executor of Mrs. Eddy's estate. In 1911, he received the degree LL. D. from Howard University, in Washington, D. C.

General Baker was an active friend as well as cousin of Mrs. Eddy, but never became a Christian Scientist. She held him in high regard, and kept his photograph on her mantel. He is mentioned at the following places in her writings: *Retrospection and Introspection* 4:7; *Pulpit and Press* 48:14; *The First Church of Christ, Scientist, and Miscellany* 135:11, 136:15, 137:17.

CHAPTER V

Mrs. Eddy's Early Years

MARY MORSE BAKER, destined to become famous as Mary Baker Eddy, was born to Mark and Abigail Baker on their five-hundred-acre farm along the Merrimack River in Bow, a rural township adjoining Concord, New Hampshire. Born on July 16, 1821, her earth-life of nearly ninety years can be divided into two periods of equal length.

During her first forty-five years she appeared to accomplish little, but during her next forty-five years she rendered to all mankind an inestimable service. As the Discoverer and Founder of Christian Science, she brought to the service of all mankind a mental and spiritual discernment and practice which has proved to be of boundless value for good uses—a renewal of Christian benefits to be attained in the present. In this way, she has won a distinguished place among the foremost women in all history. Thus, in 1932, when the National Council of Women, through the *Ladies' Home Journal*, invited American women to name the twelve greatest women leaders in the United States during the past one hundred years, the balloting gave first place to Mrs. Eddy.

Until Mary Baker was fifteen years old, she lived with her parents on their Bow farm. In 1836, they moved to another farm twenty-two miles northward and only a mile from the town then called Sanbornton Bridge. For seven years, she lived with her parents on this farm. In 1844, having become a wife and a widow, and about to become a mother, as Mary Baker Glover she resumed living with her parents there; and, after her mother's passing in 1849, she and her son moved with her father into Sanbornton Bridge. In 1853, after four years in Sanbornton Bridge, Mrs. Glover became Mrs. Patterson and went to live in Franklin, an adjacent town.

In a book published in 1837, a close observer from England said, "The Americans, particularly those of New England, look with a just complacency on the apparatus of education furnished to their entire population." [1] Mary Baker's attendance at school was impeded by ill-health, but she studied at home, as well as at school; she learned easily and she had a marvelous memory. She also continued going to school when most girls of her age would have stopped. There is ample evidence, for instance, that Mary was still attending school at the age of twenty-one. Among the schools she is known to have gone to during this period was the Sanbornton Academy at Sanbornton Bridge, a private school for young girls. Incidentally, the catalogue of the Sanbornton Academy for the three

---

[1] *Society in America*, by Harriet Martineau, Vol. II, p. 268.

terms that ended on November 21, 1842, which listed "Mary M. Baker" among the female students, also listed "Mark Baker, Esquire" as a member of its board of trustees. As Mrs. Eddy has modestly said, "All my father's daughters were given an academic education, sufficiently advanced so that they all taught school acceptably at various times and places."[1]

Furthermore, at different times Mary Baker had two excellent tutors: her educated and gifted brother Albert and one of her pastors at Sanbornton Bridge, the Rev. Enoch Corser, A. M. Mr. Corser was enthusiastic in his praise of Mary Baker. For instance, as his son has said, he once spoke of her in these terms: "Bright, good, and pure, aye brilliant! I never before had a pupil with such depth and independence of thought. She has some great future, mark that. She is an intellectual and spiritual genius."[2]

Of Mary Baker as a child or girl no photograph has been preserved. There is, however, a description of her in a letter from her cousin, D. Russell Ambrose, written in 1876. He described her as she was when about eighteen years old in these words: "A frail, fair young maiden with transparent skin and brilliant blue eyes, cheerful, hopeful, and enthusiastic." Such word pictures as these may convey more information than is likely to be furnished by a photograph. Incidentally, the color of Mrs.

---

[1] *Miscellany*, p. 310.
[2] *The Life of Mary Baker Eddy*, by Sibyl Wilbur, p. 33.

Eddy's eyes is a disputed subject, because they showed differently at different times.

Further information about Mary Baker is furnished by two groups of letters and a journal which she wrote during the period from 1835 to 1843. Some of the letters were written to her brother George; the others were to a schoolmate, Augusta Holmes. The journal was of "a trip to the White Hills in July, 1843," a trip which extended to Littleton, New Hampshire, and to Newbury, Vermont. These writings, therefore, contain direct and natural expressions of herself from the time when she was a girl of fourteen to when she was a young woman of twenty-two; hence, they contain parts of a description to be collected by inference.

One conclusion from them is that Mary Baker, even then, was acquainted with good literature. This inference is warranted by her choice and use of words; also, by her allusions to books. Other conclusions easily to be drawn from these letters are that she was an affectionate sister and a companionable friend; she was also refined and sympathetic. They imply, too, that she was a friendly person who enjoyed social contacts in a normal way. Here is an instance from a letter dated April 17, 1837: "I have since then attended a wedding with a Mr. Bartlett. He was groomsman and I bridesmaid. We had a fine time I assure you." These casual writings also show that she had an appreciation of beauty and grandeur. This trait appears in

Lake Winnepesaukee in New Hampshire—"The smile of the Great Spirit"

her accounts of trips, one of which was to Boston and Nahant, Massachusetts, in 1839. Evidently, also, she had a sense of humor, and was habitually cheerful and even happy in spite of persistent ill-health. As regards religion, these writings manifest an interest which seems exceptional now, but may not have been extraordinary at that time.

Mary Baker was brought up in an environment which was particularly conducive to religious tendencies, even for New Hampshire in the first half of the last century. Her parents were active members of the Congregational church. At Concord, when Mary was a girl, their pastor was the Rev. Nathaniel Bouton, A. M., D. D., an able minister and a famous preacher. He was a graduate of Yale College and of Andover Theological Seminary. For thirty-seven years he was a trustee of Dartmouth College. About 1830, his church was "the rallying point of the town, and the great congregation, averaging about a thousand, thronged it every Sabbath. They came from all directions, long distances, and many on foot."[1] At Sanbornton Bridge, one of her pastors was the Rev. Enoch Corser, A. M., less famous than Dr. Bouton, but equally able, and equally learned. He graduated from Middlebury College with the degree A. B., studied theology with a tutor, and received the honorary degree of A. M. from Dartmouth. Another of her pastors was the Rev. Corban Curtice, who also was a capable and educated minister. Mrs. Eddy has acknowl-

[1] *History of New Hampshire*, by John N. McClintock, p. 560.

edged indebtedness to these and other ministers on pages 31–32 of her Message to The Mother Church for 1901.

The home of Mary Baker's parents was a calling or staying place for ministers of more than their own denomination, and her parents were devotedly religious at all times. So was her grandmother. Indeed, her grandmother and her mother deserve to be described as both devout and spiritually-minded. Her father was equally devout, but his disposition was no less strict than was the current theology.

Before Mary Baker was born, her mother felt the conviction, and confided it to a devout neighbor, that the unborn child was consecrated and destined for wonderful achievements. Her father, too, regarded her as an exceptional child, different from his other children, even though they, too, made creditable records in their several ways. She began early to disclose religious aptitudes and preferences. From childhood she enjoyed religious instruction at home and at church. At an early age, she had learned to pray effectively, and at twelve years she felt impelled to dispute the current doctrine of predestination. [1]

Five of the poems in Mrs. Eddy's published poems were written in her youth. [2] Each of them, as is to be observed, includes a religious note or has a religious tone. The letters and journal just mentioned contain definite indications of Mary Baker's religious thought. In a letter dated April 6,

---

[1] *Retrospection and Introspection*, pp. 13–15.
[2] *Poems*, pp. 18, 32, 58, 60, 62.

1839, she referred to God as "the Source of all good." In a letter dated April 9, 1840, she said, "There is one who has promised to be a 'father to the fatherless,' and if we go to him, we shall indeed find consolation." In 1843, when writing in her journal at Franconia in the White Mountains, she recorded the aspiration "to contemplate all in God and God in all, even to the tender shrub that stoops to the vale so faintly shadowing forth the symbols of an invisible power—the kind tokens of Deity."

In a later letter, not dated, but probably written in 1848, Mary Baker Glover wrote to another friend: "You must not feel sad or anxious about the future. . . . I trust the future has stores of joy for you; and with life in its endless vicissitudes let us ever remember there is One 'who careth for us'—too wise to err, too *good* to be unkind. On Him you may rely, and find a Father and a friend." Alluding to her widowhood, she added, "This is my only consolation, *unworthy* as I am—and 'tis the greatest I can recommend to those I love."

Mrs. Glover's mother passed on in 1849; and her father married again in 1850. From then until her marriage to Dr. Patterson in 1853, she lived with Mr. and Mrs. Tilton at Sanbornton Bridge. Mrs. Tilton was her sister Abigail, the most affluent of her relatives. During these years, however, as allowed by different degrees of health, Mrs. Glover did what she could to earn money. She wrote for newspapers and periodicals, she conducted an infants' school for a time, and she taught in the New Hampshire Conference Seminary, a reorganization of the academy, during the absences of regular teachers.

Always fond of children, Mrs. Glover had a Sunday school class, frequently or regularly, at Sanbornton Bridge. Often it consisted of little girls. One of them, later Mrs. Martha Philbrick Weeks, long afterward wrote: "I would learn a few verses from the Bible, and after repeating them to her, she would explain them to me. She was very pretty to look at; her cheeks very red, her hair was brown curls, she had beautiful eyes. She wore a cape of moire silk. . . . Her bonnet was white straw and had a pink rose in each side, with her curls she was just lovely."

Mr. and Mrs. Tilton offered a home to Mrs. Glover, but not to her little boy. Consequently, another home had to be arranged for him, and the best arrangement that could be made placed him at a long distance, measured by the conveyances of that time. So, in 1850–1853, her circumstances included lack of dependable health, limited earnings, living in a home as a dependent, widowhood, separation from her child, and attentions from several apparently desirable suitors who might or might not fulfill the obligations of a husband and a stepfather. This period can be regarded as the end of Mrs. Eddy's early years; and, as she has said, "My dominant thought in marrying again was to get back my child." [1]

---

[1] *Retrospection and Introspection*, p. 20.

Patterson Cottage in Rumney, New Hampshire

New Hampshire Conference Seminary Buildings

CHAPTER VI

MRS. EDDY'S TRANSITIONAL YEARS

IN 1853, when Mary Baker Glover married Dr. Daniel Patterson, a dentist who had also studied homeopathy, she was thirty-two years old and an invalid. She never had been robust, and since the birth of her child in 1844 she had not been well. Dr. Patterson knew about her health; he had learned about it from her and from her father. Her condition of health, better or worse at different times, was for long periods a disadvantage to both of them, but it was not the only deterrent factor in their situation. He was capable as a dentist, and popular socially, but as the future proved he was deficient in other qualities essential to financial and marital success. Her lack of health contributed indirectly to her discovery of Christian Science; it was among the circumstances which impelled her to seek and find the one remedy for every ill and all evil.

For two years, Dr. and Mrs. Patterson lived at Franklin, New Hampshire, where and whence he had practiced dentistry before they were married. He did much of his work in Franklin, but made professional visits to other places occasionally or regularly. He put off the bringing of her child to live with them. His practice was not so prosperous as it had seemed; and instead of increasing, it decreased ominously. So, in March of 1855, they moved to North Groton, New Hampshire, a village on the edge of the White Mountains, near where her son had lived with his former nurse for several years. Here Dr. and Mrs. Patterson made a new start. Using borrowed money, he bought a dwelling, a hundred acres of land, and a sawmill. Continuing occasionally to practice his profession, he also operated the sawmill.

This venture at North Groton lasted five years, but it ended in utter failure. His creditors took all of Dr. Patterson's property. They also took property belonging to Mrs. Patterson—books, furniture, and a gold watch—which she had pledged as security for his debts. At first, at North Groton, she was allowed to see her child, but rarely. In April of 1856, he was taken to Minnesota by the former nurse and her husband, with whom he lived. After this, Mrs. Patterson did not see her son again until after he had grown up. Then, she found that he had become very different from what she had hoped he would be.

In 1860, Dr. and Mrs. Patterson changed their abode to Rumney, another village in the same vicinity. There they lived for about two years, during which he resumed his dentistry, making it more itinerant than local. Early in 1862, he got a commission from the governor of New Hampshire to distribute a fund for "loyalists" in the Southern States. From this service, or from imprisonment after he was captured by Confederate soldiers, he returned in the latter part of the same year. For a while, he lectured on his experiences in the South. Then he practiced his profession at different places, either by himself or with other dentists, until after he and Mrs. Patterson made another start together at Lynn in 1864. During these two years, she remained at Rumney for a few months, lived with her sister, Mrs. Tilton, for a time, spent several months at a "hydropathic institute," went to the drugless healer to be mentioned later, visited friends at several places, and developed her ability as a writer and speaker.

At Lynn, Dr. and Mrs. Patterson lived together most of the time from the summer of 1864 to the summer of 1866, when he again left her. In 1873, she obtained a divorce, after having resumed her former name, Glover; and in 1877, she married again and became Mrs. Eddy. Another event of far greater importance occurred in 1866, for that is the year in which she discovered Christian Science.

Mrs. Eddy's health was at its worst when she was Mrs. Patterson and lived at North Groton (1855–1860). Her condition there is attested by contemporary letters from members of her family and by statements from other people who knew her. In April of 1856, immediately after her son went to what was then far-off Minnesota, she was so sick that she had attendants by day and night. In June of 1857, when one sister went to see her, the other sister reported to their brother George's wife that "such a picture of suffering and misery is enough to break a sister's heart. .... What words can express her condition!"

During this illness or about this time, Mrs. Eddy gave the promise to God that, if He restored her health, she would devote her future years to helping sick and suffering humanity. Long after 1866, she put her initials to a statement of this vow and the further statement that she had kept it faithfully. Her health improved, but she continued far from well. Having little or no confidence in medicine, she dieted, practiced homeopathy in an amateur way, gave hydropathy a trial, and, more than all else, studied the Bible.

In 1861, Dr. and Mrs. Patterson heard of remarkable cures effected by a drugless healer at Portland, Maine, known as "Dr." Quimby. In October of that year they received from him a copy of his "circular," which appealed convincingly to her. What that particular circular contained is not known, but he issued circulars which described his method vaguely and which were evidently intended to assure the sick that he could heal them. In these circulars, he used the terms "error" and "the Truth" with reference to disease and its cure.

Mrs. Patterson resolved to call on "Dr." Quimby, but lack of money and alternating periods of depressed or improved health kept her from doing this until the autumn of 1862, when she went to him at Portland for treatment. Almost immediately, she felt a quick gain of strength; and although she continued in poor health after having a severe relapse, yet she enjoyed periods of added strength from that time. To what can this improvement, such as it was, be attributed? Either partly or wholly, it can be attributed to her confidence in him or in what she regarded as his method. Thus, in the midst of the relapse just mentioned, she wrote to a friend, "I have lost no faith, even if I am worse."

A further account of Mr. Quimby is necessary, because Mrs. Eddy has been accused persistently of having acquired Christian Science from him. Phineas P. Quimby lived at Belfast, Bangor, and Portland, Maine, from 1804 to 1866. Unlettered, he learned to be a clockmaker. When mesmerism engaged public interest, he found that it enabled him to control consenting subjects. Then, for years, he gave public exhibitions as a mesmerist. While doing this, he learned that he could, in some cases, cure disease or stop suffering. After a time, therefore, he quit giving public exhibitions and engaged in healing the sick, but he was apt to speak of his instrument in other terms than mesmerism, such as electricity.

Brief accounts by Mrs. Eddy of her experience with Mr. Quimby are in her *Miscellaneous Writings* (pp. 378–381) and *The First Church of Christ, Scientist, and Miscellany* (pp. 306–308).

Among the inquirers and patients who went to Mr. Quimby about the time Mrs. Patterson did was the Rev. Warren F. Evans, who was then interested in the mental aspect of disease and the "psychopathic" method of treatment. Later, in 1869 and 1872, he issued books entitled *The Mental Cure* and *Mental Medicine.* Mr. Evans, therefore, had a motive for considering Mr. Quimby's method both closely and sympathetically; and he expressed his opinion in the latter book. After giving Mr. Quimby credit for wonderful success, Mr. Evans summed up Mr. Quimby's method in these words: "But all this was only an exhibition of the force of suggestion, or the action of the law of faith, over a patient in the impressible condition." In a previous chapter on "The Conscious Impressible State," Mr. Evans defined it as a magnetized condition not involving sleep. In short, he found Mr. Quimby's method to be based on magnetism or mesmerism.

Another inquirer and patient who went to Mr. Quimby about the time Mrs. Eddy did was Mrs. Annetta G. Dresser. She lived in or near Portland, and had many contacts with him. Afterward, in 1882, she studied Christian Science, but she did not become a Christian Scientist. On the contrary, in 1895 Mrs. Dresser issued a small book in which she advocated his "philosophy." Hence, the following statement in her book is noteworthy: "She [Mrs. Eddy] was cured by him [Dr. Quimby], and afterwards became very much interested in his theory. But she put her own construction on much of his teaching, and developed a system of thought which differed radically from it." [1] It is

---

[1] *The Philosophy of P. P. Quimby,* p. 50.

quite true that Mrs. Eddy attributed to Mr. Quimby's method or teaching an idealism and a spirituality which it did not possess, and that Christian Science is radically different from anything practiced or taught by Mr. Quimby.

Mrs. Dresser spoke too strongly when she said that Mrs. Eddy was cured by Mr. Quimby. That he did not cure her is proved by her letters of that time. He treated her first in the autumn of 1862, probably in October, and her letters from then until after her last contact with him in 1865 show that she was frequently sick, sometimes "very ill," and that she was afflicted by her "old diseases."

The Mother Church has affidavits from a number of persons who knew Mr. Quimby in his later years and afterward became Christian Scientists. One of these affidavits is from Mrs. Emma A. Thompson, who went to Mr. Quimby as a patient at Portland in 1862, while Mrs. Patterson was also one of his patients. The following excerpts are from Mrs. Thompson's affidavit: "His treatment consisted in placing bands on his wrists, plunging his hands in cold water, manipulating the head and making passes down the body. He asked me to concentrate my mind on him and to think of nothing and nobody but him. He requested the members of the family to leave the room, as he said he could not control my mind with any one else present. As the relief came to me, he suffered greatly himself, saying that he took on my pain. . . . The only instructions ever given me by him were to concentrate my mind on him and drink water until the pain was relieved. . . . There was nothing in Dr. Quimby's method of treating disease which bears any resemblance to the teachings or methods of Christian Science. He never spoke of God to me, or referred to any other power or person but himself."

Among Mr. Quimby's last patients was a Mr. Clark, who went to him for treatment at Belfast in October of 1865. Mr. Clark's wife, Mrs. Jane T. Clark, accompanied him, and the following excerpts are from her affidavit: "The following was his method of treatment: He placed both his hands in a basin of water; then the left hand upon the patient's stomach and the right upon the top of the patient's head; he slightly manipulated both the stomach and the head. The immediate effect was as if a hot iron had been placed upon the part, and the sensation seemed to come from Mr. Quimby's hands. I myself took two treatments from him for a long-standing complaint. The treatment was as above. Upon experiencing the hot sensation I asked him: 'How did you come by this power, and what is it?' He answered definitely: 'I don't know how, nor when, nor what it is. I think it is probably electricity passing from me to my patient.' . . . He never attributed his ability to heal to God. In fact, he never spoke of God, and was not a religionist."

In law and in logic, an admission contrary to one's bias or interest has a particular value as proof. In 1930, H. A. L. Fisher, Warden of New College, Oxford, issued a book,

Mrs. Eddy's Transitional Years

Our New Religion, An Examination of Christian Science, based mainly on adverse sources, including manuscripts or notes attributed to Mr. Quimby. The following excerpts from Mr. Fisher's book are quoted, partly for the foregoing reason. In them, the word "her" refers to Mrs. Eddy.

"What exactly her book owes to Quimby remains, and will probably continue to remain, a matter of doubt: nor does it much signify. If *Science and Health* would never have been written without Quimby, Quimby would certainly never have written *Science and Health;* and in the development of Christian Science that book, and that book only, has been of decisive importance."

"Prayer, meditation, eager and puzzled interrogation of the Bible, had claimed from childhood much of her energy, so that those who met her in later times were conscious of a certain quiet exaltation, such as may come to a woman nursing a secret spiritual advantage."

"When we ask what was the inner source of her power, the answer can only be that it was religion. Upon many of her intimates she made the impression of a saint. The great ideas of God, of immortality, of the soul, of a life penetrated by Christianity, were never far from her mind."

When Mrs. Eddy was sixteen years old, in 1837, she wrote to one of her brothers concerning one of her sisters: "Martha has been very ill since our return from Concord. I should think her in a confirmed consumption if I would admit the idea, but it may not be so, at least I hope not."

These words, "if I would admit the idea," do not necessarily express the teaching of Christian Science, but they
contain as much of this Science as can be found in anything
known to have been said or written by Mr. Quimby. In
fact, all that she could have got from him, even in the general direction of Christian Science, were a few useful words
and additional proof that health depends on mental conditions and is subject to mental influences. Her experience
with him was a factor in her approach to Christian Science
only as her experience with homeopathy had been. [1]

Christian Science is not only mental; it is also and dis-
tinctively spiritual. It distinguishes as the Master did between one's God-given life and what seems to be a material
and separate existence: "It is the spirit that quickeneth; the
flesh profiteth nothing" (John 6:63). It distinguishes as
Paul did between one's God-given ability to think truly
and the false thinking which seems to come or spring from
other sources: "Not that we are sufficient of ourselves to
think any thing as of ourselves; but our sufficiency is of
God" (II Corinthians 3:5).

Indeed, Christian Science consistently and completely
distinguishes between that which can be attributed to God,
the divine Mind, the infinite Soul or Spirit, and that which
cannot pass this test. Thus, as regards its mental practice
and the opposite, Mrs. Eddy has said: "The basis of mal-

---

[1] See *Science and Health with Key to the Scriptures* by Mary Baker Eddy
152:21–15.

practice is in erring human will, and this will is an outcome of what I call *mortal mind,*—a false and temporal sense of Truth, Life, and Love. To heal, in Christian Science, is to base your practice on immortal Mind, the divine Principle of man's being; and this requires a preparation of the heart and an answer of the lips from the Lord." [1] In short, Mr. Quimby had not even a glimmer of that which is distinctive in Christian Science.

Besides the Quimby canard, other assertions and conjectures have been made as to where Mrs. Eddy got this or that for Christian Science, but all of the known facts point plainly to the conclusion that she progressed directly from the Christian orthodoxy of her childhood to the union of Christianity and its Science. As she once wrote to a descendant of her first pastor, the Rev. Dr. Bouton of Concord: "The religion that he taught and lived, I honor and love. It was the vestibule of Christian Science."

---

[1] *Rudimental Divine Science*, p. 9.

CHAPTER VII

A MARVELOUS HEALING

MRS. EDDY'S discovery of Christian Science sprang from experiences that extended through many years. Yet her marvelous recovery from an injury in February, 1866, was so important that she could and did assign her discovery to this event and the unfoldments that followed during the year.[1] She writes on page 24 of *Miscellaneous Writings*, "That short experience included a glimpse of the great fact that I have since tried to make plain to others, namely, Life in and of Spirit; this Life being the sole reality of existence." She explains also on page 26 of *Retrospection and Introspection*, "The miracles recorded in the Bible, which had before seemed to me supernatural, grew divinely natural and apprehensible."

From the summer of 1864 until 1882, except for intervals, Mrs. Eddy lived in Lynn or Swampscott, which are adjoining places. At different times during these years, she was Mrs. Patterson, Mrs. Glover, or Mrs. Eddy. In February, 1866, she lived in Swampscott at what is now 23 Paradise Road; she was injured by falling on an icy street

---

[1] See *Science and Health* 107:1; *Miscellaneous Writings* 24:7–18; *Retrospection and Introspection* 24:1–21.

near the corner of Oxford and Market Streets in Lynn. This occurred on Thursday, February 1. Her healing occurred at her home on the following Sunday, that is February 4, 1866. Many of her friends and acquaintances knew or heard that she had recovered in a marvelous way, and that she attributed this result to divine aid or prayer. They could confirm her account of her healing, and their doing this helped her to get a hearing for Christian Science.

Two witnesses have furnished further proofs in recent years. The following statement, now owned by the Longyear Foundation, is from a milkman who had customers in Swampscott in 1866. As correctly spelled, the name of the house owner mentioned was Arminius C. Newhall.

Swampscott, Aug. 29, 1920

To whom it may interest:

I was personally acquainted with Mrs. Eddy in 1866, then Mrs. Mary Patterson. She lived at that time in the house now numbered 23 Paradise Road, then Paradise Court, then owned by Mr. Armenus Newhall. Mrs. Patterson attended the Congregational Church, also, a Temperance Society which the writer also attended. She wrote and read many pieces to the meetings. By way of business the writer called at the house 23 Paradise Court every morning, seeing Mrs. Patterson quite often on the back ground of the premises. There was a fountain stoned up with granite. The writer used to see Mrs. Patterson on the wall apparently in deep thought. She would write a little while, then gaze into the water a while as if waiting for inspiration. While in those moods she wished no conversation with anybody.

In 1866, the mercury below zero, upon calling at the house

I was informed that Mrs. Patterson had met with an accident by falling on the ice and had broken her spine and would never be able to take another step alone. Two members of the same church, Mrs. Carrie Millet and Mrs. Mary Wheeler, were with her. Dr. Cushing of Lynn was the attending physician. A part of what stamped the affair so permanently on my memory was that Mrs. Millet asked me to go down to Marblehead line and inform the Minister, the Rev. Jonas B. Clark, of the accident. There being no public conveyance in those days, with the mercury below zero and a slow horse and business pung, I drove a distance of two miles. When I got back to town I was so near finished with cold I could not speak for some time. Three or four mornings after, upon calling at the house, Mrs. Millet informed me that a great change for the better had come over Mrs. Patterson. The evening before, to use Mrs. Patterson's own words, she says, "I am going to walk." Those present thought her mind wandering. She immediately pushed herself unaided to the side of the bed, placed her feet on the floor and walked to the side of the room and sat in a chair. Then she says, "This is all through prayer," it being the first time she had moved her legs without help since her injury.

A few years after Mr. Newhall sold the property 23 Paradise Road to a Mr. Pearl of Boston. Then Mrs. Patterson went to live with Mrs. Wheeler. While she was there Mr. Newhall bought the house on New Ocean Street in after years called "the Wave." Then Mrs. Patterson went there, which accounts for the reason that many people think the house on New Ocean Street is where Mrs. Patterson first demonstrated Christian Science. The next I knew of her was she lived on Broad Street, Lynn, having a large sign on the house which read "Christian Science Home" under the name of Mrs. Mary Glover.

The circumstances of which I have written are as fresh and clear in my memory as when they occurred.

Very respectfully

GEORGE NEWHALL

Where Mrs. Eddy's Healing Occurred in 1866

A Marvelous Healing

It is to be noted that Mr. Newhall does not name any date or day. The date when Mrs. Eddy fell on the ice in Lynn is fixed by an item in the *Lynn Reporter* for Saturday, February 3, 1866, as follows:

Mrs. Mary M. Patterson, of Swampscott, fell upon the ice near the corner of Market and Oxford Streets, on Thursday evening, and was severely injured. She was taken up in an insensible condition and carried to the residence of S. M. Bubier, Esq., near by, where she was kindly cared for during the night. Dr. Cushing, who was called, found her injuries to be internal, and of a very serious nature, inducing spasms and intense suffering. She was removed to her home in Swampscott yesterday afternoon, though in a very critical condition.

The following affidavit was made by a former resident of Lynn now living in Boston. Most of the persons named in the affidavit are mentioned in the biographies of Mrs. Eddy written by Sibyl Wilbur and Lyman P. Powell. As the affidavit relates, this witness, then a girl of ten years, and her mother saw Mrs. Eddy on the day of her recovery, before and after that event.

STATEMENT OF MRS. ARIETTA MANN
My mother, Mrs. Rebecca Brown (Mrs. Ira P.) and Mrs. Patterson were great friends. She used to come to our house a great deal when she boarded with the Phillipses, and she always acted the same as though she were in her own home. My parents were also great friends with the Phillipses. We lived on Essex Street, Lynn, at that time.

On the Sunday morning after Mrs. Eddy fell on the ice at Lynn, she sent for my mother (Mrs. Patterson lived on Paradise

Road, Swampscott, then). My father got the horse, and we went down around noon. I can still see her as she lay on the couch. When we were leaving, I had gone into the hall when Mrs. Patterson said, "When you come down the next time, I will be sitting up in the next room. I am going to walk in." My mother said, "Mary, what on earth are you talking about!" However, when we did go down that night (we had chicken for dinner, and mother carried down her supper), sure enough she was in the other room. And the doctor said she walked in.

Mrs. Patterson used to write a great deal; she had a leaning that way. Mrs. Miranda Rice was a patient of hers, and she studied with Mrs. Patterson. As little children will, we used to try to get Mrs. Rice's daughter Flora to tell us what Mrs. Patterson did to her mother. I knew Dorr Phillips well and Susan Oliver, his sister; also, Mrs. Winslow, Mr. Phillips' sister.

Dr. Patterson was a large man. When people went to his office to have their teeth attended to, Mrs. Patterson would often go into the office and sit beside them while the work was being done. I used to see her there, and once she sat beside me when Dr. Patterson worked on my teeth. She would say it wasn't going to hurt, and it didn't.

At that time, Mrs. Patterson was slender, with very bright eyes. She wore her hair with curls on each side of her head; there were two on each side, I think. She used to like to have me comb her curls, and I had a round stick on which I used to curl them.

I knew Dr. Eddy, too. He was short and stout; he used to wear a tall hat, and always carried a cane. They thought a lot of each other.

I was born on October 3, 1856.

Boston, Oct. 31, 1934.

MRS. ARIETTA MANN
Formerly Arietta Brown

A Marvelous Healing

Mrs. Mann's statement, like Mr. Newhall's, confirms what Mrs. Eddy has written in *Miscellaneous Writings* 24:7–18 and in *Retrospection and Introspection* 24:1–21 as to the uncommon nature of her recovery. In effect, also, Mrs. Mann confirms Mrs. Eddy's statement in the first of these citations as to the time when the healing occurred.

The physician who attended Mrs. Eddy when she was injured, Dr. Alvin M. Cushing, a homeopathist, described her injury differently at different times, but he always said or implied that she was injured severely. Probably he furnished the gist of the item in the *Lynn Reporter*. As Mrs. Eddy was informed, he pronounced her injury fatal. Afterward, he denied having said this; but her friends evidently regarded her condition as desperate when they sent for her minister.

The following excerpts are from an affidavit that Dr. Cushing gave to opponents of Christian Scientists in 1904:

On February 1, 1866, I was called to the residence of Samuel M. Bubier, who was a shoe manufacturer and later was mayor of Lynn, to attend said Mrs. Patterson, who had fallen upon the icy sidewalk in front of Mr. Bubier's factory, and had injured her head by the fall. I found her very nervous, partially unconscious, semi-hysterical, complaining by word and action of severe pain in the back of her head and neck. This was early in the evening. . . . I visited her twice on February first, twice on the second, once on the third, and once on the fifth.

In 1907, Dr. Cushing told Sibyl Wilbur that "Mrs.

Patterson was taken up unconscious and remained unconscious during the night," that "he believed her to be suffering from a concussion, and possibly spinal dislocation," that he visited her twice during the night, and that he found her "still semi-conscious" on the following morning. [1]

As Miss Wilbur has recorded on the same page, Dr. Cushing also spoke of Mrs. Eddy's recovery. "When he called again she was in a perfectly normal condition of health and walked across the floor to show that she was cured." He did not give Miss Wilbur the date of this call, but in the affidavit just mentioned he placed the last of his six calls as having been made on February 5. Mrs. Eddy's healing occurred on February 4.

Mrs. Eddy has said that the homeopathic physician who attended her in February, 1866, "rejoiced in my recovery." [2] Nobody has disputed that her quick recovery from such an injury furnished cause for rejoicing. The issue is, or was, between different explanations. If a question remains as to how or why Mrs. Eddy recovered so quickly from such an injury, the dispute is between Dr. Cushing's explanation given to Miss Wilbur, "the third decimal attenuation of arnica which he diluted in a glass of water," and Mrs. Eddy's explanation, "As I read, the healing Truth dawned upon my sense." [3] She did not take the

---

[1] See *The Life of Mary Baker Eddy*, by Sibyl Wilbur, p. 124.
[2] *Retrospection and Introspection*, p. 24.
[3] *Miscellaneous Writings*, p. 24.

doctor's medicine, having no faith in it, and what she read was a case of Christian healing from the New Testament beginning at Matthew 9:2.

In this situation, the decisive evidence is furnished by the one witness who had immediate knowledge of what actually occurred, by the other witnesses who have corroborated her testimony, and by the good results of her discovery in the lives of countless people. The Master furnished the decisive test when he said, "Ye shall know them by their fruits" (Matthew 7:15–20). Considered in the light of this test, the Christian Science movement, based on Christian Science healing and teaching, constitutes a convincing and ever-accumulating proof that Mrs. Eddy discovered this Science as she has related and recorded.

CHAPTER VIII

ASCENDING STEPS

HAVING had a wonderful healing, Mrs. Eddy sought to know exactly how she had been healed and how this healing power could become available to herself and other people in case of need. As she has written, "I knew the Principle of all harmonious Mind-action to be God, and that cures were produced in primitive Christian healing by holy, uplifting faith; but I must know the Science of this healing, and I won my way to absolute conclusions through divine revelation, reason, and demonstration." [1]

To give him the comprehension of divine law expressed by the Ten Commandments, "the Lord called Moses up to the top of the mount" (Exodus 19:20). Likewise, the action of divine Principle lifted Mary Baker Eddy's comprehension above the level of human thought when she gained the spiritual understanding which is expressed as Christian Science.

Of course, she did not attain to entire Christian Science on that Sunday in February of 1866 when she recovered from a grievous injury immediately after reading an ac-

---
[1] *Science and Health*, p. 109.

[62]

count of Christian healing in one of the Gospels. Nor did Christian Science cease unfolding to her consciousness in the latter part of the year 1866 when, as she has written, she "gained the scientific certainty that all causation was Mind, and every effect a mental phenomenon." [1] She attained to other degrees of progress before 1870 when she copyrighted her first pamphlet, and by 1875 when she finished composing the first edition of her principal work. Her further progressive stages are not so clearly marked, but they are indicated in many ways besides the additions to her writings.

Mrs. Eddy wrote her first pamphlet, *The Science of Man*, and the first edition of her principal work, *Science and Health*, by her own handwriting. As this was first printed, the pamphlet occupied twenty-four pages; as finally revised, it constitutes pages 465–497 of *Science and Health with Key to the Scriptures*. How much time she took for composing the pamphlet is not known. The first edition of the book, as she said soon afterward, required "two and a half years [of] incessant labor *seven days in a week*."

Mrs. Eddy began the actual writing of *Science and Health* in February of 1872. She sent the manuscript, except one chapter, to the printers in September of 1874, and added the final chapter during the next year. The printing took more than a year, partly because the plates

---

[1] *Retrospection and Introspection,* p. 24.

were made from type containing many mistakes, and Mrs. Eddy felt obliged to make the necessary corrections without requiring new plates. As she said in the letter containing the foregoing quotation, "I have now the part of proof reader to take or my book will be spoiled. . . . I have now to count the letters of every word I take out or insert when I make corrections." In the same letter, she described her "present lot" as including "no home to rest in" and "one room only to work in." This description could have been applied to more than one of the different lodgings which she had while writing the first manuscript of *Science and Health.*

Mrs. Eddy practiced Christian Science healing extensively, but not for long was this her sole vocation. Other duties demanded her devotion to them. As the Discoverer of this Science, she had to formulate it in her own thought, and put it into precise statement for all who would listen or read. As Founder, she had to find, prove, and continually supervise the appropriate modes by which to communicate her discovery, preserve its purity, and make it most beneficial to all who would accept and use it. All this she did as one divinely guided. "And the Lord spake unto Moses face to face, as a man speaketh unto his friend" (Exodus 33:11).

A considerable number of the cases in which Mrs. Eddy demonstrated her Science or practiced her teaching for the benefit of particular persons are related or briefly stated in

Mrs. Eddy in 1876

her published writings.[1] A few healings by Mrs. Eddy are related here as instances.

In 1867, she healed her niece, Miss Ellen C. Pilsbury, of Sanbornton Bridge, New Hampshire, of enteritis after typhoid fever. For two weeks, the patient's condition had been extreme; the attending physician had pronounced it hopeless. Within an hour after Mrs. Eddy arrived and stood by her bed, the sufferer arose and walked; four days later she traveled more than a hundred miles by the railroad trains of that time. This healing was attested in writing by Mrs. Eddy's stepmother, Mrs. Elizabeth P. Baker, by her sister-in-law, Mrs. Martha D. R. Baker, and by her nephew, Mr. George W. Baker. Influenced by opposition and ridicule, the young lady herself, however, soon ceased to acknowledge that her astonishing recovery was a healing.

During one of the periods from 1879 to 1885 when Mrs. Eddy preached in Hawthorne Hall, 2 Park Street, Boston, she healed Henry A. Littlefield of inflammatory rheumatism. He had been and was afterward a printer employed on Boston newspapers. In his eighty-sixth year, he related his healing as follows: "I was born in 1846. I was attacked by inflammatory rheumatism in my early

---

[1] See *Science and Health* 162:16, 184:27, 192:32 to 31 next page, 389:28. *Miscellaneous Writings* 69:14, 242:19. *Retrospection and Introspection* 15:13 to 15 next page, 40:4–20. *Unity of Good* 7:6–17. *Pulpit and Press* 54:28, 69:1–9. *Message for 1901* 17:11. *Miscellany* 105:7 to 12 next page, 145:10.

thirties in such form that even the bed clothing was burdensome and painful. I had heard about Mrs. Eddy's meetings in Hawthorne Hall, and at the worst stage of the belief I was taken there on a stretcher. After the service, Mrs. Eddy came down from the platform and greeted personally the small group of about a dozen people who were there. When she came to me and shook my hand and spoke to me, I felt the healing and responded by telling her that I was healed. I walked out of the hall rejoicing, and that belief never made itself real to me again."

The "small group" mentioned in the foregoing statement may have been persons from the audience who remained after the service to speak with Mrs. Eddy. Hawthorne Hall had about two hundred and twenty-five seats, and often when she preached the seats and the standing room were not enough for all who came to hear her.

About 1888, when Mrs. Eddy lived at 385 Commonwealth Avenue, Boston, a man named Carter came there to do some work. One of his legs had been injured by a fall from a building, so that he wore an iron shoe eight or nine inches high. Afterward he related his healing as follows: "I was called to Mrs. Eddy's home on Commonwealth Avenue, in Boston, to do some light work. Mrs. Eddy came into the room where I was busy, and observing my condition, kindly remarked, 'I suppose you expect to get out of this some time.' I answered, 'No; all that can be done for me has been done, and I can now manage to get around with a cane.' Mrs. Eddy said, 'Sit down and I will treat you.' When she finished the treatment she said, 'You go home and take off that iron shoe, and give your leg a chance to straighten out.' I went home and did as I was told, and now I am so well that, so far as I know, one leg is as good as the other." [1] Mrs. Eddy may have referred to this case when she wrote in 1891 that "shortened limbs have been elongated." [2] A similar healing by Mrs. Eddy was related in a letter to her from a crippled man's niece. [3] Two other quick and important healings by Mrs. Eddy were related by the beneficiary in the *Sentinel* for October 3, 1931 (Vol. XXXIV, p. 94).

From 1870 to 1882, Mrs. Eddy resided at Lynn[4]; from 1889 to 1908, she resided at Concord, New Hampshire. Hence, her active and continuous ministry in Boston was from 1882 to 1889. During this time, less than eight years, she had much else to do besides healing, and from 1885 she gave notice in the *Journal* that she took no patients. Nevertheless, even in Boston, her healing works became known to many people. For instance, the Rev. Dr. Luther T. Townsend, professor of practical theology in Boston University, although a severe critic of Christian Science as theology, and evidently not a feminist, frankly admitted Mrs. Eddy's success in healing. Thus, in 1885, he wrote:

[1] See the *Christian Science Sentinel*, Vol. VIII, p. 216, and *The Christian Science Journal*, Vol. XXIII, p. 572.
[2] *Science and Health*, p. 162.
[3] See the *Sentinel*, Vol. X, p. 912.
[4] Mrs. Eddy spent most of 1879 in Boston, however.

"But notwithstanding these criticisms upon this misnamed 'Christian Science,' fairness requires us to add that this woman, Mrs. Eddy, by her methods, is successful in healing disease." [1]

When Mrs. Eddy's mature years should be said to have begun is a debatable question. They can be dated from 1875, when she had proved to be the Discoverer of Christian Mind-healing. She had done this by her healing, her teaching, and her writing. As yet, however, she had not founded the Christian Science religion, nor had she led Christian Scientists over or through many of the hindrances and obstacles which were to beset the Christian Science movement.

---

[1] *Faith-Work, Christian Science, and Other Cures,* p. 46.

CHAPTER IX

The Sick Are Healed

WHEN Christian Science was a new subject, casual observers sometimes confused it with spiritualism. This fact explains part of the following testimony furnished in 1932 by Mrs. Alice Swasey Wool.

"In about the year of 1876 or 1877, when Mrs. Eddy was living on Broad Street, Lynn, I was living in Beverly, and was very ill with pain in abdomen, and the doctor had not been able to relieve me. Some one proposed that I go to Lynn to see the 'medium' who healed without medicine. So I went to Lynn to see her.

"Mrs. Eddy opened the door herself and invited me in. I told her what seemed to be the matter, and she talked with me a few minutes and then said, 'Now we won't talk any more.' She closed her eyes and sat with her hands in her lap for about ten minutes. Then she said, 'You will not have that trouble any more,' and I said, 'Aren't you going to rub me, or do anything?' and she said, 'You are healed,' and I was."

Mrs. Wool describes Mrs. Eddy as follows: "She was slender, had dark hair parted in the middle and waved on the side, and wore a dark dress. I was principally impressed by her eyes. They looked right through me. It would be impossible for one to lie to those eyes." Mrs. Wool never saw Mrs. Eddy again, but this healing changed her life, although she did not become a Christian Scientist until later.

At Lynn, in 1878, Mrs. Clara E. Choate was suffering from what she believed to be diphtheria. The symptoms were such as are commonly shown by a bad case of that disease. She was a Christian Scientist, and two other Christian Scientists besides herself had failed to heal her. Then Mrs. Eddy, on being called to save Mrs. Choate's life, healed her by one treatment. As Mrs. Choate afterward wrote, "Our beloved Leader, Mrs. Eddy, came to my bedside and healed me of a terrible attack of diphtheria instantly."

In 1879 or 1880, while Mrs. Eddy was living temporarily in Boston before she left Lynn permanently, her realization of a spiritual fact healed her granddaughter and namesake, Mary Baker Glover, of the material belief called crossed eyes. In 1934, the granddaughter, now Mrs. Billings, related this healing as follows:

"During the fall and winter of 1879 and 1880, when we lived at Deadwood, South Dakota, and I was three years old, my father went to visit his mother at Boston. At that time my eyes were what is termed crossed, and during his visit he told grandmother about them. According to my father, grandmother said, 'You must be mistaken, George; her eyes are all right.'

"When he returned to our home in Deadwood, and during a conversation with my mother at my bedside while I was asleep, they awakened me and discovered that my eyes had become straightened. Mother has a picture of me taken before this incident, showing my eyes crossed. This healing was often told me by my father and mother, and is at this time verified by my mother, who is with me."

When Mrs. Eddy was at Lynn, the mother of a little boy named Stanley brought him to her for healing. He had been a very perverse child, and was believed to be at the point of death from brain fever. The mother said: "I am afraid I have come too late. I think he is gone." Mrs. Eddy told the mother to leave the child with her and to return in an hour. This she did, laying him on a bed. Alone with the child, Mrs. Eddy, as she afterward said, "went to God in fervent prayer." Soon the boy sat up in bed. She took him in her arms and continued to treat him mentally. After a time he began to struggle in her arms and to say repeatedly, "I is tick; I is tick." She replied, "You are not sick, and you are a good boy." Before the mother returned, the child was almost well, and met her at the door. In a few days the last sign of the illness disappeared. Afterward the mother reported that he was a different boy. He was healed of a bad disposition as well as of a severe malady.

In November, 1884, when Mrs. Eddy lived in Boston,

a lady called on her and said, "I am blind; I have come only to say this, for I am told you take no patients because you have so much else to do." In her reply, Mrs. Eddy spoke of goodness and health as more natural than badness and disease. She also spoke of one's duty to praise God and of one's need to leave evidences material for evidences spiritual. The lady said, "I can see a little better," and went her way. Within a week she sent a message to Mrs. Eddy saying that her sight was perfectly restored.

Early in 1885, a Christian Science practitioner healed Mrs. Laura Lathrop of disorders which had made her an invalid for twenty-three years, but did not heal her of hereditary heart disease, which she did not mention to the practitioner. Later in the same year, she studied this Science with Mrs. Eddy, and went to New York City to engage in its work. About a year afterward, another of Mrs. Eddy's students told her that Mrs. Lathrop had a bad case of heart disease. So, Mrs. Eddy invited her to spend a Sunday in her home. This Mrs. Lathrop did in 1886. Afterward she recorded her healing as follows:

"When it was time for dinner I accompanied Mrs. Eddy to the dining-room, which was in the basement of the house. On returning to the parlor she ran up the stairs like a young girl. I was ashamed not to make at least an effort to do the same, but for twenty-four years I had never run upstairs. . . . This time I did go as fast as she did, but when I reached the top step I was in a sorry plight. How

I looked I cannot tell. I only knew that I was seized with one of my old attacks. . . . She gave me one glance, and then, without asking me a question, she spoke aloud to the error. We are told that when Jesus healed the sick, he spake as one having authority. . . . A few months after, I was seized with another attack, but it lasted only a moment and went never again to return. That was eighteen years ago."[1]

In many cases, pupils in Mrs. Eddy's classes were healed by her teaching. A typical instance was furnished by Eugene H. Greene, of Portland, Maine, later of Providence, Rhode Island, in her class of November, 1884. His widow, who was in the same class, has related his healing by Mrs. Eddy as follows: "During this class, Mr. Greene was healed of a hernia he had had for many years. Mrs. Eddy had previously healed him of tuberculosis."

Later, Mrs. Eddy required applicants for her classes to be in good health before entering them. The joy of being healed might keep them from getting the full benefit of her teaching, as she has explained on pages 14–15 of *Rudimental Divine Science*.

At the meeting of the National Christian Scientist Association in Chicago in 1888, Mrs. Eddy delivered an address, open to the public, at the Central Music Hall, which healed more than a few persons. One of the healings that resulted from this address, "Science and the

---

[1] *Sentinel*, Vol. VII, p. 259.

Senses," [1] or from what Mrs. Eddy said after it, was observed by Mrs. Emilie B. Hulin of Brooklyn, New York, who often related it and finally recorded it as follows:

"I was seated in the gallery near the stage, where I had a good view of the platform and the audience. I noticed a woman on crutches coming down the main aisle with great difficulty. She was seated in the front row opposite the stage. At the conclusion of Mrs. Eddy's remarks, which took for their topic the spiritual meaning of the Ninety-First Psalm, the woman referred to arose in her seat and with outstretched arms said something to Mrs. Eddy, who leaned over the platform and said something in reply which I could not hear. Immediately this woman laid down her crutches and walked out straight and erect."

After Mrs. Eddy returned to her home in Boston, she also spoke of the same healing to members of her household as one of the healings that had occurred during or following her address in Chicago.

In 1902 or 1903, Mrs. Jeannette Glick made an engagement to meet a Christian Science practitioner at the Christian Science Hall in Concord, New Hampshire, to be treated for what a physician had diagnosed as asthma and heart disease. When she arrived at the Hall, she stood in front of it with the practitioner and other Christian Scientists to see Mrs. Eddy, who was expected to pass in her carriage. When Mrs. Eddy came in her carriage, she

---

1 *Miscellaneous Writings*, p. 98.

Courtesy, Chicago Historical Society

Central Music Hall, Chicago, Illinois

greeted the group on the steps of the Hall, but to Mrs. Glick in particular she gave a look which one of the group afterward described as "long, searching, and deeply loving." Then, as soon as Mrs. Eddy had gone by, Mrs. Glick said to the practitioner: "I don't need a treatment; I am healed. Dear Mrs. Eddy greeted me with a smile, and now I am well." And the future proved that she had been healed instantly by Mrs. Eddy's compassionate reflection of divine Love.

When Miss Abigail Dyer Thompson of Minneapolis was a child, Mrs. Eddy gave her two healings at different times, which she related in the *Christian Science Sentinel*[1] and in her reminiscences.

From her babyhood, Miss Thompson was a delicate child. She was believed to have inherited a tendency to lung trouble, and physicians expressed the opinion that she would not live to maturity. Once when this disorder was especially evident, her mother, one of Mrs. Eddy's students, took Miss Thompson to call on Mrs. Eddy in Boston. As soon as Mrs. Eddy heard the child cough she gave Miss Thompson one treatment, which erased every vestige of the dreaded disease and completely freed her from the believed liability to it.

A year or so later, when Miss Thompson was again in Boston with her mother, she was stricken suddenly by an acute and severe malady of a different kind. For two

---

[1] Vol. XXXIV, p. 94.

weeks, first one practitioner and then another failed to furnish relief. Finally, at five o'clock one morning, when Miss Thompson had seemed to endure as much pain as she could possibly stand, her mother went to Mrs. Eddy's home to beseech her help. Mrs. Eddy heard the talking in her hall; and, as she afterward told Mrs. Thompson: "I said to myself, it is time for me to step in on this case and save that child. Then, hurrying back to my room I dropped into a chair and immediately reached out to God for the healing." Miss Thompson responded to Mrs. Eddy's mental work instantly. She was much better before her mother returned, and in a few days she traveled fifteen hundred miles to their home in perfect freedom.

About the year 1870, when Mrs. Eddy was staying with a friend in Chelsea, a suburb of Boston, a cripple came to the friend's door. His arms were so stiff and his legs so contracted that he was strapped to crutches. Mrs. Eddy saw him and gave him something. Hobbling to the next house, he was given permission to enter and lie down. In about an hour, he found his arms and legs loosed; he could stand erect, he could walk; he was well. And he attributed his recovery to Mrs. Eddy, for whom he inquired without knowing her name. Later, some of Mrs. Eddy's students asked her how she healed him, and she replied, "When I looked on that man, my heart gushed with unspeakable pity and prayer."

What mental and spiritual factors contributed to Mrs.

Eddy's success as a practitioner? As to this question, one can only draw conclusions from her words and works. Evidently, one factor was her absolute confidence in Christian Science as a divine revelation. For this reason and from experience, she was certain that its basic ideas can be demonstrated. Another factor was that her comprehension of particular ideas was both clear and positive. Another important factor was that Mrs. Eddy loved; she yearned to do good. Furthermore, she was certain that God is divine Love, whose law or providence is always available and is always adequate for every need. Once she wrote that "the consciousness of God as Love gives man power with untold furtherance." [1]

---

[1] *Message to The Mother Church for 1902*, pp. 8, 9.

CHAPTER X

Mrs. Eddy as a Practitioner

IN many instances, Mrs. Eddy healed persons who did not come to her as patients. Their condition attracted her compassionate and loving thought. For instance, while she lived at Lynn and was passing along one of Lynn's streets, she saw a man sitting on the sidewalk who was so deformed or crippled that his knees touched his chin. Going to him and leaning over so that her face was close to his, she said, "God loves you," and went on without waiting. Almost immediately the man arose and walked. A Christian Scientist, Mrs. Lucy Allen, saw this healing from her window. Then the man rushed to her house to inquire about the lady, the "angel," who had healed him.

Later, when Mrs. Eddy lived in Boston, she healed another deformed or crippled man. His arms seemed useless; his legs appeared to have withered. He had to be cared for, even fed. Every day during pleasant weather he was taken to the park called Boston Common in a wheel chair and left there for an hour or two. One day, as Mrs. Eddy went through this park in the midst of Boston, she saw this man in his wheel chair and talked with him; she spoke of the

Christ, and told him the truth of his being. He felt that she had helped him, and looked for her day after day in the park. She did come again, and she spoke to him in the same way. And this time he was completely healed. Long afterward, his niece related his healing in a letter that was published in the *Christian Science Sentinel* for July 18, 1908.

Such marvels may remind one of those that are recorded in Acts 3:1–16; 14:8–18. Even in the Master's work, a healing could require two treatments. See Mark 8:22–26.

Mrs. Eddy had a great love for children, and she delighted to heal or help them. In one case, a thirteen-year-old girl was a consumptive and extremely weak. Her father was the janitor of a Boston hall where Mrs. Eddy preached. One Sunday he brought the child to the hall, carried her to a seat, and left her to stay there until he could take her home. After the service, as Mrs. Eddy was leaving the hall, she saw the child and talked with her briefly according to Christian Science. She was healed immediately; her father was amazed when he came for her, as was her mother when they arrived at home. And soon the child was free from even the memory of having been sick.

In another case, when Mrs. Eddy lived on Columbus Avenue in Boston, she became fond of a neighbor's child, a little girl, who had never walked. Not seeing the child for several days, she called at her home to inquire about her. The child's mother, in great sorrow, replied that the child had been taken ill and had just died. Mrs. Eddy then asked to see the child and to be left alone with her. The mother assented reluctantly, saying that nothing could be done; it was too late. When left with the child, or with its lifeless body, Mrs. Eddy took it in her arms and began to pray. Becoming conscious only of infinite Life, Truth, and Love, she became oblivious of the material situation until the child recalled her to human surroundings by sitting up and asking for her mother. Then, when the mother came in response to Mrs. Eddy's summons, the child ran to her, enabled to use her limbs as well as restored to life.

In a number of instances, persons who exhibited common evidences of death and appeared to be dead were restored by Mrs. Eddy's practice of Christian Science. A case of restoration from death or its approximation is related in the next paragraph.

At Lynn, when Mrs. Eddy lived there, a teamster passing her house was thrown to the ground so that a heavily loaded wagon ran over him. One wheel crossed his body, crushing it. Men who carried him into her house regarded him as dead, but one of them proposed seeing whether she could do anything for him. Others spoke of an inquest as required. The commotion caused by the accident attracted Mrs. Eddy's attention; and she went downstairs to where the body was and prayed or treated silently. In a short time, estimated differently at a few minutes or half an hour, the injured man became conscious, sat up, stood up, declared he was not hurt, and walked back to his team.

At first after Mrs. Eddy discovered Christian Science, most of the people who had any knowledge of it regarded it more as a cure without medicine than a religion. The healings that she wrought, however, proved its moral and spiritual value. Many of the persons whom she healed manifested not only a change in bodily health but also a change in conduct, an improved condition of thought.

An instance was furnished by a farmer named John Scott in 1870. He had a bad case of enteritis. He had no bowel movement for two weeks, he suffered terribly, and a medical consultation gave him no promise of recovery. Mrs. Eddy healed him in less than an hour. His bowels began to act normally, he said he felt perfectly well, and he resumed work the next day. Later, his wife reported to Mrs. Eddy that Mr. Scott had also become a different man. After giving details, such as his changed attitude toward their children, she said, "Oh, how I thank you for restoring my husband to health, but more than all else I am grateful for what you have done for him morally and spiritually."

In 1868, at Lynn, Mrs. Eddy healed by one treatment a lunatic who had escaped from an asylum. As he wandered insanely, he entered the house where she had a room. His clothes were in tatters; his appearance was frightful. The mother and daughter who occupied most of the house were badly frightened. The daughter fled; the mother called for Mrs. Eddy to come. When she responded, the man raised a chair as if to strike her, but she felt a great compassion for him, and faced him without fear. Immediately he dropped the chair, fell on his knees at her feet, and began to sob. Reaching out her hand as if she were giving him a benediction, she touched his head. When he asked what she was doing, she told him she was anointing his head with oil, alluding to Psalms 23:5, and told him to go in peace. Thereupon he left the house, evidently restored to sanity. Long afterward, in 1884, this man called on Mrs. Eddy at her home in Boston to express his gratitude. He told her that he had returned to the asylum, had been discharged as cured, and had traced his healing to her. He told her, further, that he had gone to live in the West, had married, had become the father of children, and had never been insane after she anointed him as if with oil. She meant by her answer to his question, as she once said when relating this case, the anointing of Truth.

About 1878, at Lynn, Mrs. Eddy healed a little girl named Josephine Green who was ill with what the attending physician diagnosed as brain fever. Going to the home of Mr. and Mrs. C. E. L. Green to rent a room, Mrs. Eddy learned that their daughter was very sick and asked to see her. Afterward, Mr. Green related the healing as follows: "We had quite a little chat with Mrs. Eddy before she saw the child. She went into the room and stood at the bedside.

Red Rock, Lynn, Massachusetts

She took the little girl's hand, and spoke to her in a low voice. In about twenty minutes or half an hour she asked us to let her dress the child. We could not understand, but let her do so. Then she said, 'Let me take the child out.' We protested, but we had confidence in that woman. She took the child across the street and back. Although we were afraid, the child was all right the next day, and she came along all right. The doctor called the next morning and he could not understand it."

About 1882, when Mrs. Eddy moved from Lynn to Boston, she healed a young man named Hanover P. Smith, who did not hear or speak. He had been deaf and dumb from his birth, and was in his nineteenth year. He had tried to get relief by medical means; he had been in an institution for the deaf and dumb. Finally, his mother took him to Mrs. Eddy, who healed him quickly. Afterward, he became an active member of the Church of Christ, Scientist.

In 1886, while Miss Mary H. Crosby, afterward Mrs. Mary H. Mahon, was a student at the New England Conservatory of Music in Boston, an illness from which she suffered resulted in the statement from her physician that the lining of her stomach was destroyed and that she should return to her home prepared to live only a short time. Hearing of Miss Crosby's distress, a lady connected with the Conservatory recommended that she call on Mrs. Eddy, who conducted the Massachusetts Metaphysical

College in Boston, and was said to heal as Jesus did. Accordingly, Miss Crosby called on Mrs. Eddy, who listened to her story, but did not promise to treat her. In the evening of that day, however, the conditions of which she spoke to Mrs. Eddy disappeared, and Miss Crosby found herself entirely healed from them.

In 1885, Erwin L. Colman had arrived in Boston as a pupil in a class that Mrs. Eddy was teaching. His wife, Janet T. Colman, was in Omaha expecting the birth of a child. During a session of the class, he received a telegram that his wife was dying in childbirth. Mrs. Eddy saw him get it and leave the classroom. Following him, she inquired as to what he had heard, and he showed her the telegram. Then she assured him that his wife would not die, she would recover, he could return to the class. This he did; and as events proved, Mrs. Colman was healed of severe injuries at the birth. Afterwards, she had a long and useful career as a practitioner and teacher of Christian Science.

Naturally, Mrs. Eddy's discovery of Christian Science impelled her to communicate it to other people and put it into practical use for them. Necessarily, also, she began to do this without having customary rules or usages determined by experience and wisdom. Moreover, the methods adapted to the introduction and propagation of a new teaching are not necessarily adapted to the later stages of its development and progress. Therefore, the customary rules or usages now followed by Christian Scientists for the propagation of Christian Science are not to be inferred particularly from what Mrs. Eddy did in the beginning of the Christian Science movement.

Most of Mrs. Eddy's practice for particular persons occurred during the twenty years, 1867–1886, that followed her discovery of Christian Science. All of the healings related in the foregoing paragraphs are from that period. She never made practice for particular persons her chief occupation. Always she devoted her thought chiefly to her own obligations as Discoverer, Founder, and Leader. From 1885, she gave notice in *The Christian Science Journal* that she would not take patients. Yet, she was the instrument for many healings after that.

In the historical files of The Mother Church there is a letter to Mrs. Eddy dated December 9, 1904, from a lady who described herself as "one of the lepers who has come at last to give thanks for his healing." Presumably, she alluded to the ten lepers whom the Master healed, as related in Luke 17:11–19, of whom one returned to give thanks. She continued: "You healed me many years ago of a loathesome disease with just a word. The trouble has never returned. Words fail to express my gratitude for that healing." She also inclosed a check, which Mrs. Eddy returned with an appreciative letter.

On November 9, 1908, about two years before she passed on, Mrs. Eddy revived Calvin A. Frye, a member of her household, when he appeared to have died. In the evening of that day, another member of the household found Mr. Frye in his room on a lounge unconscious. She called two other members of the household, and all three of them tried to revive him. His eyes were closed, he appeared to have no breath or pulse, and he gave no sign of life. Not getting any evident result from their work, they decided to inform Mrs. Eddy. When one of them did this, she said, "Bring him to me;" which they did. Then she said, "Do not touch him; leave him to me." Then, besides what she did mentally, she commanded him to awaken from his false dream, to arouse himself, to wake up. After an interval, he began to breathe, he opened his eyes partly, he moved his head from its limp position on one of his shoulders. Becoming conscious gradually, he began to speak. Before long, he arose from the chair on which he had been carried, and walked to his room unaided. One of the three witnesses remained with him that night, to be at hand if needed, but he was not; and in the morning Mr. Frye resumed his accustomed duties as usual.

The Principle and method of Christian Science healing are fully stated in Mrs. Eddy's published writings. To them she gave her most careful and helpful thought, not only once, but often. Her letters and the reminiscences of persons who heard her speak contain other sayings on this subject, but they do not extend her teachings nor do they compare with her published works in either interest or value. The following quotations are among the most helpful sayings by Mrs. Eddy that the present writer has found in her letters or in her attested oral statements.

"Now I name a need that is above all others to ensure the perpetuity of the present success of Christian Science and its continued advancement, namely, a higher and more practical *healing*."

"There is one infinite Life, and that Life is eternal, and that Life is my life."

CHAPTER XI

Contacts with Mrs. Eddy

IN a letter dated April 26, 1900, concerning a portrait to be painted from photographs, Mary Baker Eddy wrote: "My thoughts form my face and its expressions; hence, these vary and no photographer has caught the expression of my best thoughts or the thought of my best expression. . . . Of this I am sure, that my works, not my face, must declare me." Although the human face may index the human self, the countenance is most indicative when seen in action and as part of a larger mental picture. Therefore, the following accounts of contacts with Mrs. Eddy are offered for their informative value.

For a period from 1877, Mr. and Mrs. Eddy occupied two floors of a house in Lynn, Massachusetts, and let the other floor to a tenant, Mrs. Elvira Newhall, whose cousin, a young man named J. Henry Jones, boarded with her. In 1931, Mr. Jones wrote as follows: "I have very distinct recollections of Mrs. Eddy. She was a very attractive woman with a lovely face and a very good figure. Her complexion was unusually fine, and she had a good color. She looked different from the ordinary run of people. There was something about her that made me call her a saintly-looking woman. She was rather reserved. I never saw her when she was not calm and serene. I do not remember that she ever talked to me of Christian Science. We all knew that she spent her time writing. I have never become interested in Christian Science, but whenever anyone has said anything to me against Mrs. Eddy I have defended her and have declared her to be a saintly woman and a wonderful woman."

The following statement is from Mrs. Caroline D. Noyes, of Chicago, one of Mrs. Eddy's students: "In 1883, I attended a lecture by Mrs. Eddy at her home in Boston. Her subject was 'Belief, Faith, and Understanding.' She was beautiful in face and figure; her grace, dignity, and freedom of expression were very remarkable. Her perfect ease and her choice of language were very striking. Her exquisite taste in dress and her immaculate neatness in appearance were also very noticeable. Her fine, expressive, dark eyes, violet I should call them, beamed with kindness and intelligence. Altogether, she was most attractive and engaging. From so fine and ladylike an individual, one would hardly expect the strong and forceful way she displayed at times, both in conversation and in her lessons. She had an affectionate and endearing manner, but her strong ways also created an unfailing confidence in her ability to establish the great work she did. When I first knew her, she was nearly sixty years of age but appeared not over thirty-five or forty."

The following account is by Mrs. Helen Andrews Nixon of Boston, who studied Christian Science with Mrs. Eddy in 1889: "In the autumn of 1888 Mr. Nixon, our son Paul aged six, and I called upon Mrs. Eddy by appointment in her home on Commonwealth Avenue, Boston. A few months' study of *Science and Health with Key to the Scriptures,* and many remarkable demonstrations of healing by means of its teachings, had convinced me that its author must, of necessity, be a good and very wise woman, but I was not anticipating the impression Mrs. Eddy's presence made upon me. Standing beside her as she greeted me, I felt I was in the presence of one who was like Jesus. That she understood me better than I understood myself and could read my thoughts I felt sure. I felt like a little child and was not afraid to have her see my innermost thoughts, for such inexpressible tenderness and love radiated from her. No other human being had I ever met like her."

In 1889, Mrs. Eddy retired for an interval to Barre, Vermont. In 1933, Mrs. Eva Rogers Travers recorded her contact with Mrs. Eddy there in part as follows: "One of the loveliest and most distinct memories of my childhood is my meeting with Mary Baker Eddy when she stayed at Barre. At that time, I was a child of twelve years. My father was a very strict religious man, and he was firmly convinced that Mrs. Eddy was an agent for the devil. Because of this, I became very curious about her.

"One Sunday afternoon, I obtained permission to take a walk, and immediately made my way, with two other little girls, to the house which Mrs. Eddy occupied. She was reclining in a hammock under the trees, reading a book. When she saw us, she arose from the hammock and walked toward us. As she approached us, I was conscious of the beautiful picture she made. The expression in her eyes and the lovely smile she gave us are unforgettable. She talked to us very kindly, asked our names, and talked about the flowers which were growing in the yard. Finally, she picked a small bouquet for each of us, and we went home. The memory of those few moments we spent with Mrs. Eddy and of the beautiful impression she left upon my thought has never been forgotten."

In 1892, Joseph H. Leishman, of Boston, was chief of construction for a firm of builders and realtors who arranged for him to consult Mrs. Eddy as to whether the buildings on the land now occupied by the original edifice of The Mother Church should be torn down so as to preserve the materials or so as to merely get rid of the old buildings. He was loath to keep the engagement, because he was exceedingly busy and because he did not expect from it anything practical or worth-while. In 1931, Mr. Leishman related this interview as follows: "Mrs. Eddy was rather dainty in appearance, was of medium height, and was straight as an arrow. Her big eyes penetrated one deeply as he looked into them. I had imagined that I would meet a woman whose years lay heavily upon her. Instead, I met one with the sweetness, spirit, and complexion of a child. Her personality was charming; her face radiated happiness and love. Her knowing eyes, twinkling and sparkling as she spoke, helped me to conclude that she quite understood what she was listening to and what she herself was talking about. Her requests were brief and to the point; her explanations were as clear and distinct as they possibly could be. And so the lasting impression that I got of Mrs. Eddy was one of a cultured, an educated, and a well-balanced woman.

"She asked me to consider most thoroughly the matter before us, and to make a concise and exhaustive report, as she wanted the information to be useful for the future as well as for the present. She also asked me when she might expect the report. I said that my office force was occupied with other matters, and that I was all alone. Quick as a flash her answer came, an answer that has been ever with me throughout the years and has done much to shape my course: 'Mr. Leishman, you are never alone!' So affected was I by her words that I could not at once reply. Finally, I did say that the desired report would be in the hands of my principals within ten days and in her possession immediately thereafter." Later, Mr. Leishman became a Christian Scientist.

In 1895, Miss Mabel Hill was a teacher in a church school at Concord, New Hampshire, and wrote occasionally for Boston newspapers. A letter of introduction to Mrs. Eddy enabled her to get an interview which lasted two hours. In 1928, Miss Hill narrated this experience in part as follows: "Mrs. Eddy was dressed in a rich plum-colored cashmere, the basque (we wore basques in 1895) was trimmed with ermine at neck and wrists. A brooch at the throat was the only ornament. She was dainty in costume, dainty in figure, with a beaming penetrating smile that won the heart. Innocence of guile seemed to pervade her person, and yet withal she was a most dominating personality. Just how or why, I could not grasp. I recognized, without doubt, but without understanding, that I was in the presence of an unusual woman, one whose restraint and yet cordiality, whose serenity and yet childlike gaiety, were a natural product of a large nature—one who was hourly receiving strength and inspiration from Powers unseen by my girlish eyes. The two hours that I had spent with that remarkable woman stirred my faith, lifted my ideals, and brought me poignant happiness. The visit broadened my outlook on life and the relation between the visible and the invisible."

In 1896, William Elmer Crofut, now a manufacturer at Cleveland, was an aspiring newspaper man on the staff of the *Syracuse Post*, now *Syracuse Post-Standard*. He had gone to Concord, New Hampshire, to see the young lady who soon became his wife. Although a young reporter, he had interviewed national and international personages. So he asked for and got an interview with Mrs. Eddy. Mr. Crofut called at the appointed time, and she did not keep him waiting. The gist of his story, written recently by request, follows.

"Disturbed as I was that my presence might be an intrusion, her kindliness at once removed every trace of my embarrassment. She was queenly and yet gracious. She bade me be seated. She sat close to me in a low, comfortable chair. She was dressed in all black, a well fitted black silk, I think, and high at the neck. Her face was rich in natural color for one of her years. Her eyes were large and luminous. They were dark, perhaps black. Her hair was abundant and pure white. The only ornament was a diamond brooch in the form of a cross, and of goodly size. It appeared to me more as an emblem of her eternal faith than as an ornament. This cross of pure white diamonds was outstanding on her dress of black. It added quite something to that atmosphere of spirituality which seemed to encompass her. I knew then and I know now that I was in the presence of an extraordinary person. It was as though here was one who had fasted—had been in long periods of prayer and solitary communion with her God and her Christ and that something of the heavenly, something of the great spiritual life eternal, had settled upon her.

"She said that in those years spent in seclusion and prayer she had asked to be 'guided to that Mind that is in Christ.' She had found that it was the human will that

[94]

was the origin of disease and that the divine Mind was the Healer. She felt that she was only obeying the voice and command of her Master, which was 'to go into all the world and preach the gospel and heal the sick.' She asked that I take back to my home her message of love and gratitude to those devoted followers there. I never saw her afterwards. I have felt always that this was my greatest interview. Her presence has always been with me. Her name is surely enrolled among the greatest religious leaders of all time."

In 1899, Miss C. Lilias Ramsay and Miss E. Mary Ramsay, of Edinburgh, Scotland, saw Mrs. Eddy in her carriage at Concord, New Hampshire, twice, heard her speak to members of The Mother Church in Boston, and had an interview with her at her home. The following impressions of Mrs. Eddy were written by Miss C. Lilias Ramsay: "As the carriage passed us we had a good view of Mrs. Eddy, and we were greatly struck by the beauty of her features and the dignity of her pose as she sat erect and stately. 'Why,' I exclaimed, 'she is a queen!' No portrait that we had seen at that time had given us any true impression of her beauty, grace, and dignity. She was wearing a purple velvet bonnet showing a profusion of white curls, and had an ermine tippet over her shoulders. We continued our walk, and then on returning we met the carriage again. This time we were nearer, and Mrs. Eddy saw us and bowed and smiled so charmingly that I said to my sister, 'If she is a queen, she is a queen whose meanest subject would not fear to approach her!' Her whole figure, seen more closely, conveyed to me the word 'gentleness.'"

Frank E. Irwin was a lumber salesman who called on customers at Concord, New Hampshire. He had been benefited by Christian Science, but retained a critical attitude toward Christian Scientists and toward Mrs. Eddy in particular. One day in 1903, he was in a customer's office at Concord when Mrs. Eddy came in to speak about a contract connected with the building that she was giving to First Church of Christ, Scientist, of Concord. Mr. Irwin did not see her closely then, but he heard what she said, and was strongly impressed by the direct and intelligent manner in which she handled this business. An hour afterward, he saw her face to face as her carriage stopped where he was in a Concord street. His account of this meeting follows: "I heard a voice behind me, I looked around quickly, and looked into Mrs. Eddy's face. I never want to, and know I never shall, forget the look on her face. Any ideas derogatory to Mrs. Eddy or Christian Science vanished into thin air, and I know from that moment on I was a better man. It seemed a turning point in my life when I was thrown into contact for the first time with absolute purity."

Mrs. Mary Henderson Toms, of Knoxville, Tennessee, one of many Christian Scientists who heard Mrs. Eddy speak from the balcony of her home in 1903, has related this experience thus: "At the appointed hour, Mrs. Eddy appeared on the upper verandah and walked slowly out on the balcony, where she stood silently for a few minutes looking into the upturned faces. Her expression was one of great tenderness and yearning love. Mrs. Eddy's voice was beautiful, clear, distinct, and musical. It also had a spiritual quality that is indescribable. She was beautiful; her features looked like chiseled marble. She must have been about eighty-two years of age. To me, she did not look sixty. She was slender and very erect, and she walked gracefully, in a queenly manner. There was nothing rigid or feeble about her posture; she had a buoyant step. Her eyes looked dark and luminous. I wish I could describe her expression that day. To me, it was one of victory over the material world; it was also an expression of holiness and unselfish love. The spiritual exaltation that followed my visit to Pleasant View stayed with me for years."

In 1904, Mrs. Mary Lloyd McConnel, of Ilkley, England, was at First Church of Christ, Scientist, of Concord, New Hampshire, and was standing nearby while Mrs. Eddy spoke from her carriage. In 1935, Mrs. McConnel described Mrs. Eddy as follows: "She was lovely, old and yet so very young. Indeed, ageless seems the best word to employ. Her hair was white, her complexion as fair and smooth as that of a young child. Her eyes were marvelous. You could not possibly tell what color they were. They were just full of light."

In 1900 and in 1908, Mrs. Ella Berry Rideing, of France, saw Mrs. Eddy in her carriage at Concord, New Hampshire, and in her home near Boston. Concerning these occasions, Mrs. Rideing has written: "As I gazed into her eyes, I knew for the first time in my life what it meant to express spirituality. I was healed spiritually and morally, and experienced a great uplifting—a desire to be useful and to serve the Cause of Christian Science. I saw in Mrs. Eddy's face such sweetness and selflessness and purity that I wanted to be useful in my life, and I gained an entirely different outlook on the world.

"The last time I saw Mrs. Eddy was in 1908, at Chestnut Hill. She was seated in the bay window, in the glow of the sunset. It was a beautiful picture, with Mrs. Eddy's profile framed in the glow from the sky. Oh, the sweetness and spirituality and selflessness of her thought! She radiated it."

William R. Rathvon, later a member of The Christian Science Board of Directors, was Mrs. Eddy's corresponding secretary for over two years (1908–1910), and he contributed the following paragraphs for this chapter:

"In enumerating the graces which characterized Mrs. Eddy during the time when I was in daily association with her at Chestnut Hill, I would name her faculty of putting at their ease all with whom she came in contact. On occasions, I have talked with visitors waiting for an appointment with her who were extremely apprehensive and uneasy over the prospect of speaking with her for the first time, but who, after a few moments in her presence, were completely composed and serene.

"I have noticed, too, that in conversation with her one would be incited to voice only the good, with a clarity and understanding far beyond his ordinary ability. She seemed unconsciously to radiate intelligence that was reflected in a degree by those to whom her thought was directed in an interview, yet never was there any indication or suggestion of anything weird or uncanny about her. She was just a lovable, womanly human being, possessing traits and proclivities that were sublimated to an extraordinary degree through her recognition of spiritual realities—omnipotence, omniscience, and omnipresence.

"She was inclined to be brief, if not curt, with those who would undertake to impress her from a selfish motive with the profundity of their knowledge of metaphysics or familiarity with the letter of the Scriptures. On the other hand, I have repeatedly seen her take pains to make clear some elementary phase of the truth of being that was puzzling to the sincere student."

William P. McKenzie, a member of The Christian Science Board of Directors since 1932, has held important positions in Christian Science service for many years. He was in Mrs. Eddy's last class, 1898, and his personal acquaintance with her began in 1894. The following paragraphs are by Mr. McKenzie:

[99]

"In April, 1910, I last saw Mrs. Eddy and conversed with her. I was soon to lecture in the British Isles, Holland, France, and Germany. While making a parting call on members of the household, with no expectation of seeing the Leader, she sent for me to come to her office and we were alone for a brief visit.

"She appeared as one who had been through conflict, showing evidence thereof, yet remaining victor. Her first question was, 'Did you know me?' My whole heart went out to her in gratitude as I replied, and once more I saw the light from her eyes which made her face shine, as I told her of my appreciation and affection. When I told her about the call to lecture abroad which I had now accepted, she smiled and said that it was all well, and that I was ready for the task.

"Immediately I began to tell her of the welfare of the Publishing Society. I spoke of the many puzzling problems which had come up in our work so greatly enlarged in scope with the issuing of a daily newspaper and how much we had wished her both to advise us and to direct us—how we had asked her for this help a good many times, but she had not elected to give it and so to the best of our ability we had to seek earnestly for the guidance of Mind. Once again I saw her rare smile as with deep earnestness she said to me, 'That is just what I wanted you to do.'

"There must have been a silence for a time. I seemed in that quiet to newly discern her purpose that all of us in the movement should be actually manifesting an obedience to God similar to her own. A very brief conversation followed. She sent loving greetings to the family just as in her letters she would thoughtfully do. She spoke of the work that engaged her time and sped me on my way with her blessing.

"I know that as I sat quietly in Mrs. Eddy's presence for the last time, I gained a new sense of the word patience as I realized her rich kindness to me and her love for mankind. In the sixteen years of our friendship she had revealed to me the Christianly patience of the mother guiding the child with happy friendliness and good humor, rebuking mistakes with a clarity which produced not resentment but enlightenment. But her teachings are an open book for the whole world, and those who in humility receive the teaching can prove it for themselves and others."

CHAPTER XII

Mrs. Eddy as an Author

FOR Christian Science to fulfill its divine purpose, it must become known to mankind; for its purpose is fulfilled to the extent that human thought is brought or kept in accord with divine Principle. This Science, therefore, had to be discovered by a person who could both comprehend it clearly for herself and communicate it effectively and exactly to other people. So it was providential that Mary Baker Eddy could and did exert and develop both of these powers. More attention, however, has been given to the first of them than to the second, and there are a number of interesting facts which help to explain Mrs. Eddy's exceptional power to express spiritual verities.

At the age of seven, Mary Baker aspired to write a book, and resolved that she would. After a few years, she confided this intention to her brother, Albert, who promised to help her become a writer. This he endeavored to do, as opportunities occurred, and he was a fluent speaker as well as a capable writer. Long after she had issued a book of exceeding importance to mankind, and after she had become famous for connected reasons, Mrs. Eddy counted her early intention to write a book as one among a few of the most determinative facts of her entire history.

In her youth, two of Mary Baker's teachers were especially helpful to her in a literary way. They were Professor Dyer H. Sanborn, author of Sanborn's Grammar, and Miss Sarah J. Bodwell, principal of the Sanbornton Academy. Miss Bodwell gave particular attention to Mary Baker's literary development, and once encouraged her by saying, "You will some day be a distinguished author." This attention and prediction Mrs. Eddy remembered gratefully in her last years.

The article on Mary Baker Eddy which begins on page 99 of *New Hampshire Women*, a book of biographical sketches published at Concord in 1895, includes the following excerpts: "Attending the old Academy at Sanbornton, at sixteen years of age, she began a successful literary career. Her *Science and Health with Key to the Scriptures* is the textbook of Christian Science, now in its ninety-seventh edition. A distinguished LL. D. writes: 'The author of *Science and Health* wields more power with her pen than any other writer at this period.' . . . Her interpretation of Scriptures, being more spiritual than is common to the age, met with strenuous opposition, but she has maintained throughout an exalted Christian character, laboring only for the upbuilding of a full and perfect religion."

Other persons besides her kin and her teachers must have helped Mary Baker to develop the power to express thought in words. For seven or eight years, when she was a girl, she listened frequently to a famous preacher, the Rev. Nathaniel Bouton, of Concord. Then for six or seven years, she often heard another effective speaker, the Rev. Enoch Corser, of Sanbornton Bridge. His son, S. B. G. Corser, has left this record: "As Mrs. Eddy's pastor—and for a time teacher—my father held her in the highest esteem. In fact, he considered her, even at an early age, superior both intellectually and spiritually to any other woman in Tilton, and greatly enjoyed talking with her. . . . I well remember her gift of expression which was very marked, as girls of that time were not usually possessed of so large a vocabulary."

Naturally, also, there are other factors besides human aptitude and training to be considered as accounting for Mrs. Eddy's ability to communicate her discovery to mankind. Her ability to expound Christian Science sprang directly from the divine source of the discovery itself; and among human factors, one of the most effective was her awareness of its transcendent value. This fact has been noticed by disinterested observers. For instance, the following excerpts are from *The Story of Religion as Told in the Lives of Its Leaders,* by Charles Francis Potter, a book published in 1929.

Mary Baker Eddy "is the most compelling figure in American religious history."

"No one but a prejudiced bigot can deny her credit

for having made available to hundreds of thousands of sufferers a method of healing which literally gave them new life. The reason why she spake with authority and not as the scribes was because she was sublimely conscious of the fact that she had a message of great worth for mankind."

Mrs. Eddy was an accepted and popular author long before she discovered Christian Science. From her youth, she contributed poetry and prose which was welcomed by the editors of newspapers and magazines. Later, they were willing to pay for her writings. Not nearly all of her writings have been found or can be identified, for they were not always signed. But the following are among the publications in which poetry or prose by Mrs. Eddy has been found: the *Belknap Gazette*, the *New Hampshire Patriot and State Gazette*, the *Portland Daily Advertiser*, the *Portland Daily Press*, the *Lynn Reporter*, the *Connecticut Odd Fellow*, the *I. O. O. F. Covenant*, the *Freemasons' Monthly Magazine*, and *Godey's Lady's Book*. Two of her poems were reprinted in *Gems for You*, a collection of selected verse published at Manchester, New Hampshire, in 1850, and again at Boston, in 1856.

Mrs. Eddy also delivered lectures on current topics of public interest. As an author, she chose a wide variety of topics, usually moral, religious, political, or social. Occasionally, she wrote fiction; for instance, "Emma Clinton, or a Tale of the Frontiers" in the *I. O. O. F. Covenant* for

August, 1846. Another interesting fact is that Mrs. Eddy chose the modern title "Way-side Thoughts" for a series of articles from her pen which appeared in the *Portland Daily Press* during the latter part of 1863 and the early part of 1864.

For most of her writing on Christian Science, Mrs. Eddy had no aid from a critic or editor; she had no other help than that of a proof reader. In certain instances, however, she asked competent persons to render particular services. She did this in 1885, for the sixteenth edition of *Science and Health,* when she employed the Rev. James Henry Wiggin to compile an index and to criticize the text. Later, she employed him again to propose marginal headings for the fiftieth edition of the same book and to criticize the text of another book.[1]

Mr. Wiggin was a retired minister who had become a proof reader for the University Press, which did Mrs. Eddy's printing. As she employed him to criticize some of her writings, he helped her to anticipate difficulties on the part of readers and to make her meaning clear to all of them. That Mr. Wiggin did not claim to have done more than this for Mrs. Eddy is related by William Dana Orcutt of the University Press on pages 52 and 53 of his book, *In Quest of the Perfect Book.*

For many years, Mr. Orcutt attended to the business of the University Press with Mrs. Eddy. Therefore, he

---

[1] *Miscellany*, pp. 317–325.

had many opportunities to form direct impressions of her during his calls at her homes near Concord and Boston; and he has recorded these impressions in the book just mentioned. The following excerpts are from pages 53 and 54:

"The characteristic about Mrs. Eddy that impressed me the first time I met her was her motherliness. She gave every one the impression of deepest interest and concern in what he said, and was sympathetic in everything that touched on his personal affairs."

"At first one might have been deceived by her quiet manner into thinking that she was easily influenced. There was no suggestion to which she did not hold herself open. If she approved, she accepted it promptly; if it did not appeal, she dismissed it with a graciousness that left no mark; but it was always settled once and for all. There was no wavering and no uncertainty."

"To many her name suggests a great religious movement, but when I think of her I seem to see acres of green grass, a placid little lake, a silver strip of river, and a boundary line of hills; and within the unpretentious house a slight, unassuming woman,—very real, very human, very appealing, supremely content in the self-knowledge that, no matter what others might think, she was delivering her message to the world."

In 1901, when again revising *Science and Health with Key to the Scriptures*, Mrs. Eddy availed herself of aid from two Christian Scientists—two of her own students: Mr. Edward A. Kimball and Mr. William P. McKenzie. Expert in literary usage, they were also versed in the subject of her writing. Besides criticizing the marginal headings and the text, they corrected or verified quotations and selected testimonies for the chapter entitled "Fruitage." For their work on the text, she gave them the following instruction in writing: "First be sure that you gain my meaning, and then preserve it strictly throughout the book. If you hesitate as to my meaning, send the number of the page and the sentence to me, and I will make it plain." All of her letters or notes to them during the progress of this work were consistent with the foregoing words.

In 1906, Mark Twain (Samuel L. Clemens) argued in print that Mrs. Eddy was not the author of all the writings attributed to her because, in his opinion, no author could have used the different literary styles which he found in them. He allowed enmity to displace his habitual good humor and common sense. This attack, however, furnished the occasion for an article written by Mr. Kimball in which he described the literary service rendered for Mrs. Eddy in 1901: [1]

"Since its first edition she [Mrs. Eddy] has been making changes in 'Science and Health' constantly, for the purpose of rendering her meaning clearer and of easier

---

[1] *Cosmopolitan*, May, 1907.

comprehension on the part of the reader. The book has improved, and it is because *she* has improved it. A few years ago, prior to the casting of new plates for the printer's use, she decided to make several hundred verbal changes. I assisted in this work, and I know that with the exception of possibly five or six instances every one of the changes was made on her own initiative and by her own hand."

In an article on Mary Baker Eddy in the *Living Church* for October 1, 1932, one of her biographers, the Rev. Dr. Lyman P. Powell, has furnished another complete reply to Mark Twain's attack by speaking of Mrs. Eddy's versatility as a writer. On this topic, Dr. Powell concluded as follows:

"By actual count in her published writings hers was a vocabulary of 18,000 words, which makes her second in vocabulary only to Shakespeare among those who have written in the English tongue."

In his biography of Mark Twain, Albert Bigelow Paine has recorded several interesting facts. Mr. Clemens once wrote to a friend, "Somehow I continue to feel sure of that cult's [Christian Science's] colossal future." Mr. Clemens admired Mrs. Eddy, even if he also disliked her. He frequently acknowledged that humanity owed to her a deep obligation for Christian Science healing. Mr. Clemens also said, "Closely examined, painstakingly studied, she is easily the most interesting person on the planet, and in several ways as easily the most extraordinary woman that was ever born upon it." [1]

Mrs. Eddy had a distinctive literary style long before she discovered Christian Science. And from the time when the inspiration gained by her discovery gave her the corresponding power to explain her new subject, her literary usage can be easily recognized. For instance, one of her earliest expressions of Christian Science, which she then called Moral Science, was a letter of about a thousand words in the *Lynn Transcript* for February 3, 1872. Although she was then only beginning to find the verbal modes best adapted to her new subject, yet the following excerpts from that letter can be easily recognized by students of Mrs. Eddy's final usage. The capitalization may have been the printer's.

"Moral Science belongs to God, and is the expression or revelation of love, wisdom and truth. It reaches the understanding, first, through inspiration, and secondly, by explanation. Those who receive it must obey its requirements if they would understand it. . . ."

"All that is good, God has made, but all that is not good, man has sought out through many inventions. Moral Science enables us to determine good from evil, and to destroy the latter. . . ."

"To be able to control our bodies by the soul, *i.e.* through God, is to be able not to let our bodies control us

---

[1] See Vol. II, pp. 1075, 1076, and Vol. III, pp. 1186, 1187, 1271.

through the senses. Moral Science teaches this soul-control, and just in the proportion to the greater or less extent that this truth is understood, will be the success or non-success of its students. . . ."

This letter, which was intended mainly to distinguish her method from mesmerism, is believed to have been the first public statement of her teaching by the Discoverer and Founder of Christian Science. Incidentally, it announced that she was preparing a book on this subject.

A fact connected with Mrs. Eddy's literary style, and with her ability to employ diverse literary forms, is that she was a natural poet. She often thought in poetic terms when writing either poetry or prose. A related fact is that she often thought in figurative terms. Both of these habits contributed to the beauty of her writings.

There are other points to be considered by either an observer or a student who would appreciate Mrs. Eddy's literary style. The most important of them is that Christian Science, as its name indicates, is the Christian religion interpreted in an original manner and applied in a scientific way to the overcoming of evil with good throughout the range of human thought. Her choice and use of words ought to be judged in view of her purpose and the nature of her task.

A connected but distinct point is Mrs. Eddy's preference for Scriptural terms; to an extent, such terms are indispensable for writing on Christian Science, but she often chose them by preference. A typical instance of Mrs. Eddy's use of Biblical terms is furnished by the following sentence from her *Message to The Mother Church for 1901* (pp. 1 and 2): "As Christian Scientists you seek to define God to your own consciousness by feeling and applying the nature and practical possibilities of divine Love: to gain the absolute and supreme certainty that Christianity is now what Christ Jesus taught and demonstrated—health, holiness, immortality." In this sentence, the Scriptural words "divine," "love," "health," "holiness," and "immortality," plus a capital letter for one of them, are woven into a practical rule which elucidates the meaning of the Scriptural word "God." Furthermore, this use of such words, besides the reference to Christ Jesus, has given to the entire statement a clarity and a sacredness which might not have been attained by the use of other terms.

Literary method is akin to literary style, and it, too, can be found in Mrs. Eddy's writings. A notable example is her insistent reiteration of fundamental ideas. More than mere repetition, this method involves presenting a thesis from different approaches, with different applications, or in different terms, until the fundamental thought has been completely expressed and effectively sustained. Some such method has been employed by the greatest of moral protagonists in the history of the world.

The Master said (John 5:30): "I can of mine own self

do nothing: as I hear, I judge." Mrs. Eddy could have said, As I heard, I wrote. And she has spoken to this effect in *The First Church of Christ, Scientist, and Miscellany* (114:23 and 115:4). Referring to *Science and Health with Key to the Scriptures*, she said at one of these places: "I have been learning the higher meaning of this book since writing it."

CHAPTER XIII

REMINISCENCES OF MRS. EDDY

THE many pictures of Mrs. Eddy portray her external appearance at particular moments during her more than eighty-nine years. These mechanical or skillful records also convey impressions concerning her actual self—her mental and spiritual selfhood, but they do this differently to different people, according to their diverse experiences and perceptions. Evidently, therefore, a description by a capable observer may be more informative than a photograph or portrait.

In May or June of 1888, Miss Emma McLauthlin, an art student, began to attend the services of the Church of Christ, Scientist, in Boston, while Mrs. Eddy was its Pastor and occasional preacher. In November of 1888, Miss McLauthlin was a pupil in a class taught by Mrs. Eddy, and at her request Miss McLauthlin sat near Mrs. Eddy, so that she could study her face while she was teaching, preparatory to painting a portrait of her from life. After the class, Miss McLauthlin felt that she needed a greater knowledge of technique before undertaking such a work. Seven or eight years later, Mrs. Eddy told her that the time had passed for a portrait from life. Miss McLauthlin has, however, painted a word picture of Mrs. Eddy, as a preacher and as a teacher, when her age was sixty-seven.

The following is Miss McLauthlin's description of Mrs. Eddy as a preacher. "My first impression of her as she appeared on the platform [of Chickering Hall] was of a slender, graceful figure with great dignity, yet modesty of bearing, and having a beautiful face which seemed to radiate love and gentleness. Though her voice was not loud, her enunciation was so distinct that not a word was lost."

The following is Miss McLauthlin's description of Mrs. Eddy as a teacher. "Her gown was of purple velvet with a touch of creamy lace at neck and wrist; her hair was dark brown with not a gleam of silver threads, parted and softly waved. . . . Her coloring was as delicate as a tea-rose petal, flushing with a deeper rose when she became animated in discussion. Her nose, rather large and dominant, indicated great strength of character, as did the mouth, which, though firm and well chiseled, was of exceeding sweetness when she smiled. But who could describe her wonderful eyes! They were large and deep-set, with beautiful lines in brow and orbit, while the pupils were so large and dilated so with her varying emotions that they gave me the impression of very dark brown eyes, though many years later . . . their color seemed a deep blue. But the expression of her eyes was indescribable, kindling with earnestness, sparkling with a ripple of humor, stern with rebuke, beaming with love and compassion, or luminous with visions unseen by our eyes, with every changing mood their beauty became more apparent. Her face was instinct with refinement, purity, love, and wisdom."

The following accounts of Mary Baker Eddy are offered for their informative value.

In 1886, Miss Anne Dodge, daughter of General Grenville M. Dodge, who was famous as a soldier and a builder of railroads, went to Mrs. Eddy for Christian Science healing. Miss Dodge's homes were then in Council Bluffs, Iowa, and New York City. In 1888 and 1889, she received Christian Science teaching from Mrs. Eddy in the Massachusetts Metaphysical College. Afterward, Miss Dodge practiced Christian Science in Denver, New York, London, and Washington. She has related her first interview with Mrs. Eddy as follows:

"When I was about sixteen years of age I had been ill for two years of a disease my doctors said was incurable and which was most alarming to my parents. After a premature adolescence, a normal physical function had ceased and I was anemic. I had been given electrical treatments, and my mother had taken me to famous baths in Germany and in other parts of Europe. After returning from Europe, my mother and I heard of a woman who had not walked for eighteen years and had been healed through Christian Science. My mother knew her family. Then my mother took me to Boston to Mrs. Eddy for treatment. After a week, mother got an appointment for me, and we went to Mrs. Eddy's home, where she received me in her office or library. I had not cared much about going, as I felt so ill. My first thought on seeing her was what a spiritual woman she was and what wonderful eyes she had. Her curly hair at that time was still dark. She sat in an easy armed chair, and invited me to sit opposite her. She impressed me as being very sweet, loving, and tender. Her part of the interview, which lasted an hour or longer, was more mental than audible. She put her hand over her eyes, and I thought she was praying. At first I felt rather restless, and then I felt it was all right to be there. I looked around the room at the pictures and so on. Very soon I had a wonderful feeling of peace and I felt uplifted. The flesh didn't seem real to me any longer. It was a wonderful experience. At the conclusion of her mental work she said, 'Now, my dear, you may get up and you are perfectly well.' She also said she would see me again soon. That evening the illness vanished for all time. It never came back. Mrs. Eddy had healed me in one treatment."

Edward P. Bates, a business man of Syracuse, New York, received Christian Science teaching from Mrs. Eddy in the Massachusetts Metaphysical College in 1887 and 1889. So did his wife. Later he held important positions in the Christian Science movement. He was a member of The Christian Science Board of Directors, President of The Mother Church, and for a time a Trustee of The Christian Science Publishing Society. In his reminiscences,

Mr. Bates has given the following account of Mrs. Eddy and her teaching in 1887:

"Vividly I remember how I anticipated meeting Mrs. Eddy and hoped to receive a great benefit from her teaching. I was not disappointed. Soon after we entered the reception room of the College, Mrs. Eddy appeared. I was amazed. She was a different type of woman to me. My mother was a spiritually-minded woman from the old standpoint, but to her had not been granted the revelation which came to Mrs. Eddy. I realized then, and more clearly realize today, that to understand a character such as hers demanded close study. I saw a lady slight in form, her sweet face lighted by beautiful, lustrous eyes, and nut-brown hair with scarcely a touch of white. With all this she combined the grace and poise of a perfect gentle-woman. Back of this was that intangible entity that I could not fathom. I have studied Mrs. Eddy's character ever since, and today, after nearly twenty-five years of acquaintance with her, I realize how much I have yet to learn regarding her character and the scope of her work.

"We enjoyed the class, and were rejoiced to be there. Her teaching unfolded the Scriptures day by day. Although she taught only from the chapter Recapitulation in *Science and Health*, she opened the consciousness to a wide field of thought, breaking down old theological barriers which had prevented us from comprehending the truth. The members of the class grew to love her from day to day as she expounded her teaching. She was considerately kind to all, pausing for us to assimilate her statements and comprehend them. If members of the class hesitated or were backward about accepting her statements, she dealt with them with the utmost kindness till they saw and accepted the truth of her statements. Thus, she won their entire confidence and respect."

Mrs. E. Blanche Ward, of London, one of the earliest and most prominent of the Christian Scientists in the British Isles, had an interview with Mrs. Eddy at Concord in 1898. Mrs. Ward has related this event thus: "In 1898 I had the privilege of visiting our Leader, Mary Baker Eddy, and a long talk with her at her home, Pleasant View. As she appeared to me, Mrs. Eddy was the very embodiment of vitality, grace, poise, and naturalness. Her clear complexion, youthfulness, symmetry of form, and kindliness of manner made a lasting impression upon me. Her interest in all that pertained to the work and workers in England showed her tender care for all her flock. She addressed me tenderly as 'Child'; she spoke, also, of her love for little children and of the way in which they helped her. In conversation, her simple, direct way of getting to the very heart of the subject under discussion was remarkable. Nothing was left unfinished; every point was dealt with satisfactorily. I was on the point of leaving the house when Mrs. Eddy ran down the steps with the ease and agility of a young girl, remembering that she had something more to say to me. Immediately before, during, and after my visit, I experienced a deep and marvelous peace. Never before had I experienced such an entire absence of fear, and I received abiding inspiration from her every word."

The Rev. Irving C. Tomlinson of Boston met Mrs. Eddy in 1897, and was a member of her last class in 1898. By her appointment, he was First Reader of the branch church at Concord, New Hampshire, for seven years. He was one of the three members who composed the first Publication Committee of The Mother Church, and was one of the five members who first composed our Board of Lectureship. Mr. Tomlinson was also a member of our Leader's household, serving as one of her secretaries, during the three years of her residence at Chestnut Hill. The following excerpts are from his reminiscences.

"Mrs. Eddy delivered her last address in Christian Science Hall at Concord on February 26, 1898, in her seventy-seventh year. The auditorium was crowded to the doors by citizens of Concord, as well as followers from Boston, New York, Philadelphia, Montreal, and elsewhere. Mrs. Eddy appeared at her best. No Bossuet, Wesley, or Whitefield ever seemed more in his rightful place than did the Leader of Christian Science in the Concord pulpit. She took as her text the ninety-first Psalm, which she read without glasses. She spoke for three quarters of an hour with no manuscript or notes, freely and spontaneously.

Her voice was resonant, every word had its proper value and every thought its right inflection. So natural, so artless was her delivery that the thought of her listeners was centered not upon the messenger but upon her God-inspired message. The speaker lifted her hearers into the realm of Spirit, inspired them with strength, and convinced them of the truth of her words. Her lucid presentation showed Christian Science to be based on the Bible, and that he who accepts the teaching of the Scriptures cannot consistently deny the truth of Christian Science.

"A word only must suffice here for Mrs. Eddy's work in healing. In the presence of any need, she was always the most scientific practitioner. She was serious but not severe. She was decisive, explicit, and scientific. She firmly rebuked the error, declared the healing truth, and lovingly called upon the sufferer to manifest his true selfhood. Her cures were for the most part instantaneous."

In 1901, Miss Emilie Hergenroeder, of Baltimore, was a Christian Scientist and a portrait painter, who painted a portrait of Mrs. Eddy from photographs. Not satisfied with the result, she went to Concord, New Hampshire, to see Mrs. Eddy in order to produce a portrait that might be satisfactory. Miss Hergenroeder related her interview as follows: "Being a very young Scientist, I had no idea what it meant to see Mrs. Eddy. Nevertheless, my sister and I started to Concord filled with great expectations to see the great woman who gave the wonderful book, *Science and Health*, to the world. We arrived at our destination, but were told by a member of her household that it would be impossible for us to see Mrs. Eddy; one had to make such appointments weeks ahead. We returned to the hotel and packed our trunks to leave the next day, much disappointed. The next morning, to our surprise, a messenger delivered a note telling us to be at Pleasant View at 1.30 o'clock, as Mrs. Eddy wished to see us.

"My first impression of her is indescribable. I expected to see a tall, handsome woman, almost masculine. It was a small figure which arose from beside the desk where she had been working. She was dressed in black silk, with the famous diamond cross on her breast. She greeted us with outstretched hands. Her great eyes were smiling so kindly as she said how sorry she was she could not see us the day before, but that she did double work to be able to see us that day. She carried her head, with her beautiful white hair, very erect, and had a calm, aristocratic bearing, and the charm of expressing much tender, motherly affection. We were deeply impressed. My sister, who was quite ill with a very severe cold, was instantly healed in Mrs. Eddy's presence."

Afterward, Miss Hergenroeder painted the portrait of Mrs. Eddy which hangs in her last home.

In 1909, I was the First Reader of The Mother Church and a Trustee of The Christian Science Publishing Society. Previously, I had accepted other opportunities to serve

Mary Baker Eddy and The Mother Church. In that year, at her request, I prepared a legal paper for her to sign. Having an appointment to present it to her, I went to her home near Boston, accompanied by a notary and a witness. She greeted us cordially, listened to my explanation of the paper, examined it briefly, and executed it. After thanking the notary and the witness, she asked me to remain. Then, after some preliminary words, our Leader spoke to me for a short time on organization in relation to Christian Science. All that she said evinced her thought that the Church of Christ, Scientist, The Mother Church and its branches, is a permanent institution, essential for the propagation, protection, and usefulness of her discovery.

Closely observed, Mrs. Eddy was comparatively slender and slight. Yet her expression and speech betokened strength. One could easily see that her mental and spiritual selfhood was not to be measured by her physical stature. At this particular time, she was attired in a gray house dress, quite plain in style. She was dressed as if for work. Her manner during the first part of the interview was that of a person who knew what she had planned and only needed to be assured that the paper to be signed would carry out her intention. During the rest of the interview, she sat at ease, but erect, and spoke as one having experience and intimate knowledge of her subject. She spoke as the able Leader of a great movement who instructed the officers of her Church as occasions required.

CHAPTER XIV

MRS. EDDY'S LATER YEARS

IN February of 1889, Mrs. Eddy achieved a notable success by delivering a lecture on Christian Science in New York City, where insidious opposition had produced a dangerous situation. Delivered in Steinway Hall, after a notice of only twenty-four hours, her lecture was heard by over a thousand people. When she had been introduced, the audience listened with deepest attention while she discussed six aspects of Christian Science or subjects connected therewith. After the lecture, she was obliged to return to the stage for nearly an hour, while many persons expressed appreciation and thanks in exchange for a kindly greeting to each of them. This lecture, following another in Chicago which has been mentioned elsewhere, can be said to have completed a series of constructive measures designated to propagate and protect genuine Christian Science.

In June of 1889, Mrs. Eddy changed her residence from Boston to Concord, New Hampshire, near the places where she had lived as a child, girl, and young woman. As reasons for this change and its incidents, she spoke of desiring to live apart from the world, of transferring many tasks to others, and of taking more time for her writings. As events occurred, however, although she enjoyed a degree of respite as well as retirement, and the Directors of the Church of Christ, Scientist, assumed a larger responsibility, yet she continued to be the active Leader of the movement.

For over two years after she retired to Concord, Mrs. Eddy devoted all available time to her writings. Besides revising several of her minor works, she produced a new book, her autobiography entitled *Retrospection and Introspection*, and gave an important revision to her principal work (the fiftieth edition of *Science and Health with Key to the Scriptures*). In his review of this edition, the Editor of the *Journal* predicted that it would "mark an epoch in the Christian Science movement." As seen from the present time, the fiftieth edition appears to have been a thorough revision, which added about forty pages of text.

During the next several years, much of Mrs. Eddy's thought was given to founding The Mother Church, as The First Church of Christ, Scientist, and to developing the Christian Science organization as a whole.

If the friends and foes of Christian Science, if interested and disinterested persons, can be said to agree on any point, it is that Christian Science has an excellent organization. Its excellence is often acknowledged and even applauded by disinterested onlookers. Nevertheless, the fitness and efficacy of the modes of action formulated for the Christian Science religion can be fully appreciated only by active participants in its work. Yet, from all points of view Mrs. Eddy's achievement in this regard deserves unstinted praise. In moderate terms, her acts as the Founder of Christian Science, from the time when a distinct Church for this religion became necessary, can be described as evincing the highest order of religious statesmanship.

Mrs. Eddy furnished a striking instance of constructive ability and wisdom in 1895, when she recommended readings from the Bible and *Science and Health* of prepared Lesson-Sermons instead of personal sermons. This plan, adopted throughout the Christian Science denomination, has proved to be a great success, not only for The Mother Church, but also for the branch churches. In particular, this plan has saved the Christian Science gospel from dangers and weaknesses incident to personal ministries; carefully chosen readings from the Bible and the Christian Science textbook continually furnish interesting and instructive sermons which conform to an invariable standard; while the invitation at Wednesday evening meetings for "experiences, testimonies, and remarks on Christian Science" (*Church Manual*, p. 122) extends an ample opportunity for helpful forms of personal speaking.

In Mrs. Eddy's life, 1898 was an outstanding year. Besides ordinary work in that year, she instituted The Christian Science Board of Education, The Christian Science Board of Lectureship, The Christian Science Publishing

Mary Baker Eddy

Society as it exists now, the *Christian Science Weekly*, soon to be named the *Christian Science Sentinel*, and she taught a large class which was both her first class since 1889 and the last of all her classes. Any of these subjects is important, but only one of them can be chosen for part of this chapter.

The *Christian Science Sentinel* appears to have been conceived by Mrs. Eddy on June 22, 1898. In a letter of that date to the Editor of *The Christian Science Journal*, Judge Septimus J. Hanna, she said that she saw no other way to meet a certain plot than to have "a weekly folio sheet." The date lines of this letter concluded as follows: "At 4 A.M. was at work, and still am."

Like the *Journal* (*Miscellaneous Writings*, p. 4), the *Sentinel* began in Mrs. Eddy's thought as a newspaper. In a letter dated August 20, 1898, to one of the Trustees of The Christian Science Publishing Society, William P. McKenzie, she said, "The dignity of our cause and the good of the students demand of us to publish a weekly newspaper." In another letter to Judge Hanna dated January 19, 1899, Mrs. Eddy wrote as follows: "Sentinel is the proper title for our Weekly. . . . Also let me prophesy 'Sentinel' and the motto with it describes the future of this newspaper. It will take that place and must *fill it* when numerous periodicals of our denomination are extant." The next issue of the new periodical bore its present name, together with its present motto from the Master's words:

"What I say unto you I say unto all—WATCH." Therefore, the words "Sentinel" and "watch" mark the permanent position of this periodical among the Christian Science periodicals.

The first volume of the *Christian Science Sentinel,* which began on September 1, 1898, differed notably from the same periodical today. At first, it had only eight pages, including advertisements, and it had no cover. As a general rule, news occupied the first two pages. Most of the news was in brief paragraphs headed "Current Events" or "Items of Interest." Beginning with the nineteenth number, there was a department headed "Questions and Answers." A few of the answers were signed by Mrs. Eddy, but most of them were not signed, and were written by the editors. She supervised the new periodical closely, even giving attention to details connected with paper and printing. Addresses, articles, and answers to questions by Mrs. Eddy which were in the first volume of the *Sentinel* are reprinted as she revised them in *The First Church of Christ, Scientist, and Miscellany,* on pages 103–108, 124–131, 131–133, 148–151, 151–154, 184–186, 187–191, 210, 238, 239, 244–246, 256, 299–301, 338, and 339–341.

In July of 1899, one of the items just cited, Mrs. Eddy's Message to The Mother Church on June 4, 1899, furnished the pretext for a series of sensational suits by a former member of The Mother Church. Having been expelled in 1896, this former member became an active opponent of

Christian Science. Incidentally, she became an exceedingly unfair critic of Mrs. Eddy, even though Mrs. Eddy had consistently endeavored to help her. In May of 1899, this former member's hostility culminated in an extremely unjust article in a magazine. Pursuing the same course of action, she based her suits on the claim that Mrs. Eddy referred to her as "the Babylonish woman," and so on, in the Message just mentioned. [1] Lasting more than two years, this litigation ended when one of the suits was brought to trial and the court directed a verdict for Mrs. Eddy at the close of the plaintiff's evidence. The litigation was commenced and conducted in the most sensational manner, the plaintiff's lawyer being no less aggressive than herself. Mrs. Eddy's calmness and courage during this difficult time was evinced in many ways, but particularly by the following message, evidently intended for all Christian Scientists, which appeared on the editorial page of the *Sentinel* for August 3 and 10, 1899: " 'Peace be still!' our Father is at the helm. Mary Baker Eddy."

One of the counsel for Mrs. Eddy and the other defendants in the suits just mentioned was Samuel J. Elder, Esquire, of Boston, who afterward represented Mrs. Eddy and other Christian Scientists in other cases which will be mentioned in another chapter. In the course of this service, extending about eight years, he had more than a few consultations with her and received many letters from her.

---

[1] *Miscellany* 125:29.

For this reason, and for the reason that Mr. Elder was an exceptionally intelligent man, as well as an eminent lawyer, the opinion he formed of Mrs. Eddy has a particular interest. It has been recorded in his biography by his daughter.[1] Miss Elder relates that her father was often asked what he thought of Mrs. Eddy, and that he invariably replied that he thought her "an unusual and brilliant woman." Miss Elder also relates that her father never failed to tell a story about Mrs. Eddy—an incident connected with the last case in which he represented her. Before the trial of this suit, she called a consultation of her lawyers, and found that they agreed to take a certain position which she regarded as unwise. A full discussion made no change. After they left her, she sent for Mr. Elder, told him that they were wrong, and obtained his promise that he would ask the other lawyers to reconsider the question. "So they went over all their arguments again. The result was that they reversed their decision, followed the lines insisted upon by Mrs. Eddy, and during the trial it became indubitably clear that she had been right." This incident occurred in 1907, about three and a half years before she passed on.

In the same year, Mrs. Eddy granted interviews to well-known journalists, including William E. Curtis of the Chicago *Record-Herald* and Arthur Brisbane of the New York *Evening Journal* and the *Cosmopolitan Magazine*. Conclusions formed by these men deserve to be quoted,

---

[1] *The Life of Samuel J. Elder*, by Margaret M. Elder, pp. 200–202.

Mrs. Eddy's Home in Chestnut Hill

because they were disinterested, and because long experience had trained them to estimate the ability and character of particular persons. Their reports of these interviews cannot be fully quoted here, but the following excerpts are indicative. Mr. Curtis said, "I have never seen a woman eighty-six years of age with greater physical or mental vigor." Mr. Brisbane used these words: "It is quite certain that nobody could see this beautiful and venerable woman and ever again speak of her except in terms of affectionate reverence and sympathy."

In January of 1908, Mrs. Eddy removed from Concord to a suburb of Boston. For one reason, this change would facilitate communicating with her executives, and quicker communications with them were to be essential soon. For at least six years, she had contemplated starting a daily newspaper. In 1902, when about to install and instruct a new editor of the *Journal* and the *Sentinel*, she wrote in a letter, "Until I start a widespread press, we should have in Boston a born editor." The editor, Mr. Archibald McLellan, whose training as such began in 1902, became, in 1908, the editor of "a widespread press," for in that year she founded and made him the editor of a daily newspaper adapted to the needs of all mankind—*The Christian Science Monitor*. The establishing of the *Monitor*, Mrs. Eddy regarded as one of the greatest of all her steps.

Mrs. Eddy lived at Chestnut Hill for nearly three years —January 26, 1908, to December 3, 1910—and she continued attending to her important functions to the end of this time. For instance, in 1908, she abolished the Executive Members and the Communion season in The Mother Church. The continued vitality of her thought is also indicated strikingly by the instruction for practice now to be found on page 242 of *The First Church of Christ, Scientist, and Miscellany*. This instruction was first printed in the *Christian Science Sentinel* for September 3, 1910 (Vol. XIII, p. 10) and *The Christian Science Journal* for October, 1910 (Vol. XXVIII, pp. 485–486). The following sentences illustrate the quality of this writing: "You can never demonstrate spirituality until you declare yourself to be immortal and understand that you are so. Christian Science is absolute; it is neither behind the point of perfection nor advancing towards it; it is at this point and must be practised therefrom."

CHAPTER XV

Mrs. Eddy as a Teacher

BEFORE she discovered Christian Science and began to teach this subject, Mary Baker Eddy had experience as a teacher of other subjects. Besides conducting an infants' school for a short time, she had taught frequently or regularly in a Congregational Sunday School, and she had taught occasionally in the place of absent teachers in an academy, the New Hampshire Conference Seminary. She had also spoken and written on topics of public interest during the years preceding her discovery of this Science. These activities furnished a certain amount of preparation for teaching Christian Science. She depended directly, however, upon divine Mind, not only for her comprehension of this subject, but also for her ability to communicate it effectively. A member of her first class in Christian Science, Samuel Putnam Bancroft, 1870, has said, "At all times she seemed conscious of a wisdom beyond her own."

One of the first problems of the first teacher of Christian Science was to choose the best methods for teaching this subject. During 1867–69, when not otherwise occupied, Mrs. Eddy taught pupils one by one and for indefinite times. In 1870, she began to hold classes and give them a course of twelve lessons. From the first, she based her teaching on the Bible and on written texts which she supplied. Thus, from experience and divine guidance she adopted "class instruction" (personal instruction to classes varying in size, based upon the two textbooks of Christian Science—the Bible and *Science and Health with Key to the Scriptures*) as a permanent part of Christian Science methods. This adoption is now witnessed by Articles XXVI–XXX of her *Church Manual*, including the following part of Article XXVII, Section 5: "No member of this Church shall advise against class instruction."

The greatest of all teachers could say, "The word which ye hear is not mine, but the Father's which sent me." [1] Mrs. Eddy could say this, too. Jesus also said, "Take heed therefore how ye hear." [2] Mrs. Eddy likewise sought to make sure that "however little be taught or learned, that little shall be right." [3] Thus, she commended "the simple sense one gains of this Science through careful, unbiased, contemplative reading of my books," [4] and she made provisions in her *Church Manual* to the effect that the Bible and her writings shall be the criterion for teaching and learning Christian Science. [5]

---

1 John 14:24.
2 Luke 8:18.
3 *Retrospection and Introspection* 61:28.
4 *Miscellaneous Writings* 43:12.
5 Article IV, Section 1; Article XII, Section 2; Article XXVI, Section 6.

Mrs. Eddy as a Teacher

Mrs. Eddy did most of her teaching from 1875 to 1881, and from 1881 to 1889. One of these periods was before, the other was after she instituted the Massachusetts Metaphysical College. After 1889, she taught only one class. It was taught at Concord, New Hampshire, in 1898. In a few instances, however, she gave diplomas to members of her household who had been under her personal instruction. (See *Church Manual*, Article XXVII, Section 1; Article XXX, Section 6.)

The purpose of the Christian Science educational system, as Mrs. Eddy conceived it, is to "secure a thorough preparation of the student for practice." [1] Of her teaching to a particular class, no complete record or report ever was made. She never consented to the taking of notes, and in fact she forbade it. The Mother Church has, however, a good many reminiscences from members of her classes containing accounts of them.

Mrs. Jennie E. Sawyer (Mrs. Silas J. Sawyer) of Milwaukee was in classes taught by Mrs. Eddy that began on December 27, 1883, May 13, 1884, and October 4, 1886. Referring to the first of these classes, Mrs. Sawyer has written as follows: "Mrs. Eddy at this time was past sixty years of age, but was well-preserved and beautiful, not so much because of physical charm, as because there was discernible an inward light or reflection of thought that shone through her countenance. One felt drawn to a better life

---

[1] *Miscellany* 245:8.

just from being in her presence. She was also attractive and kind in her manner, and most considerate in guiding the thought of the pupils away from argumentative beliefs to the acceptance of infinite Mind's power and presence. Sometimes material and mortal arguments occupied hours before a higher light dawned on consciousness. This was not a large class, most of them not paying; and it lasted three weeks, including an intermission. The class members were of different church affiliations, and it was astonishing that such a mixture of thought could be brought into unison on so vital a subject as one's Christian faith, but at the close of the class we 'were all with one accord in one place.' She asked me what I would do with the thought she had imparted. I answered, 'I am filled with wonderful Truth. I do not know what I am to do with it.' Then she said, in the most convincing way, 'You are going to heal with it.' "

Miss C. Lulu Blackman, of Lincoln, Nebraska, whom Mrs. Eddy taught in 1885, has recorded this experience in part as follows: "When she entered the classroom, the members of the class rose intuitively and remained standing until she was seated. She made her way to a slightly raised platform, stood before us, and faced the class as one who knew herself to be a teacher by divine right. Then she lifted up her eyes in prayer, and all, with one accord, spoke the Lord's Prayer. But we distinctly heard these words from her, 'Our dear Father, which art in heaven.'

After this prayer, Mrs. Eddy took her seat and the students resumed theirs. As she began to speak, many of them opened notebooks and began to write. Instantly she said, 'Put up your notebooks.' Some of the students covertly began again to make notes, but she detected this, and repeated the command, 'Put up your notebooks.' She made no explanation of this requirement, but I have always blessed her for it because her impartations transcended the medium of words. Throughout the class, she effaced the sense of her personality apart from God so plainly that she thought, spoke, and acted from the standpoint of her oneness with the Father."

Mrs. Annie M. Knott of Detroit and Boston, for many years a prominent Christian Scientist and a member of The Christian Science Board of Directors, was in classes which Mrs. Eddy taught in February, 1887, and October, 1888. In after years Mrs. Knott had a number of interviews with Mrs. Eddy.

Referring to the latter class, Mrs. Knott has written as follows: "When our dear teacher entered the classroom, I felt that she was the most beautiful person I had ever seen in my life. She was a picture of strength, youthfulness, beauty, and joy, and she continued radiant and beautiful during the class. Before Mrs. Eddy's first lesson began, one of the members of the class placed two roses on the teacher's little stand. When she entered, she took them up and said, 'How beautiful they are. The world is more beautiful to me than to anyone else who lives in it because I see more of God reflected in everything.' "

Mrs. Knott has written further: "On October 5, 1892, I attended a meeting in Boston called for the purpose of carrying forward the organization of The Mother Church. The meeting was held in Steinert Hall, 62 Boylston Street, where fifty-seven persons, myself among them, signed the roll of membership. After the meeting, I was one of several of our Leader's Normal students who were invited to visit her the next day at her home, Pleasant View. The interview lasted for nearly two hours. Before saying good-bye to us, she said, 'If you, my dear students, could but see the grandeur of your outlook, the infinitude of your hope, and the infinite capacity of your being, you would do what? You would let error destroy itself.' I am sure of this quotation, because I wrote it down immediately on going back to the hotel where I was staying."

Mr. and Mrs. Edward A. Kimball, of Chicago, were in three of Mrs. Eddy's classes, March, 1888; March, 1889; November, 1898. The first two were Primary classes; the last was a Normal class. In her brief reminiscences, written in 1919, Mrs. Kimball recorded a few of her recollections of Mrs. Eddy as follows: "Like everybody else I was greatly impressed by the dignity and majesty of her appearance. I doubt if I can make it clear to a listener the wonderful impressions received when she introduced us to the new understanding of God. In 1889, we were greatly interested to see how very much like the first teaching the second teaching was. Almost every person has some episode or recollection that lives with him all his life, and I think that our meeting with this woman and the wonderful understanding that came to us then is like nothing else I have ever known."

Miss Jennie L. Bryan, of Peoria, was in a Primary class that began on September 17, 1888, and included eleven men and thirty-three women. Miss Bryan has written as follows: "Mrs. Eddy's gentleness, her tenderness and love, and her patience reminded me of the Scriptural narratives of our great Master, as did her sternness. Her absolute unwillingness to pass over an error, her severe rebuke of an error, her keen discernment of the mentality of the different students in that large class, and her manner of handling each one was something very wonderful to me. I have never ceased to be grateful for her loving consideration and patience in my own case, and I have learned much from it.

"Each day Mrs. Eddy went round the class with questions at least once. No student was excused from giving an answer. If an answer was incorrect, the question usually passed to the next student, but sometimes she gave a correction or rebuke. A very apparent vein of humor was also stamped indelibly upon my mind. At the close of the class Mrs. Eddy gave us the privilege of meeting her afterward and talking with her privately if we wished to do this."

Miss Mary Alice Dayton, of Boston, was a member of the last Primary class, March, 1889, that Mrs. Eddy taught in the Massachusetts Metaphysical College. This class, of which there is an account on pages 279–282 of *Miscellaneous Writings*, included sixty-five students, nineteen men and forty-six women; it also included pupils from previous classes, as well as new pupils. The new pupils were given front seats.

The following excerpts are from Miss Dayton's reminiscences: "My first sight of Mrs. Eddy was when she entered the classroom after all were seated. She sat on a slightly raised platform with Dr. E. J. Foster-Eddy, who supplied her with a list of the pupils one by one. This enabled her to address each one of them personally. Three days were given to asking each member of the class, What is God? Sometimes she asked this question in other words, such as, What is your present thought of God? On the fourth day she said, 'Now we must turn our attention to the opposite of God, not to make a reality of it but to understand its modes and to reduce it to nothingness.'

"Near the end of the class, our Leader read the Master's command to the twelve disciples (Matthew 10:5–13), and gave an interpretation for each of its parts. I had read the Bible from childhood, but this was the first time I had ever heard it read so understandingly. At the end of the class she said, 'You are going out to demonstrate a living faith, a true sense of the infinite good, a sense that does not limit

God, but brings to human view an enlarged sense of Deity.' " [1]

Miss Mary Brookins, of Minneapolis, sometime a member of The Christian Science Board of Lectureship, was in a Normal class taught by Mrs. Eddy in May, 1888. "That class," Miss Brookins has written, "was a loosening of the earth ties and a gleam of heaven, harmony, such as I had never imagined possible. One day during class we had an instance of our dear one's keen sense of humor. She had been lifting the veil of matter so that we almost felt that there was none, when a student leaned forward and said, 'But, Mrs. Eddy, if we had such a realization as that, when we were giving a treatment wouldn't the patient disappear?' Then we saw how our teacher could laugh. Finally she said, 'Don't you worry, my dear, when you get such a realization as you are thinking of, it will be you who will disappear, not the patient.' "

From 1892 to 1921, Judge Septimus J. Hanna filled important posts in the service of The Mother Church. During ten years of this time he was editor of *The Christian Science Journal*. At the same time, Mrs. Hanna was its associate editor. They were also together in Mrs. Eddy's last class.

In the *Journal* for December, 1898 (Vol. XVI, pp. 588–590), there was an account of this class, evidently written by one of its members, and presumably by Judge Hanna.

---

[1] *Miscellaneous Writings* 282:1.

The following quotation is from this article: "At the appointed time the first lesson began, lasting for two hours; and on the day following, the second and last was given, which lasted for nearly four hours. Only two lessons! but such lessons! It were futile to attempt a description or review. Only those who have sat under this wondrous teaching can form a conjecture of what these classes were. The Decalogue and Sermon on the Mount were brought before the class, not in epitome, but in marvelous elaboration. The whole Bible, in verity, was held up in vivid review, and its mighty, yet simple and practical, spiritual import, illustrated in language of superb clearness and picturesque beauty,—faultless in symmetry, majestic in the depth of its spiritual significance. To say that this teaching lifted one Heavenward—Godward—that it sank deep into the consciousness of all present, is only feebly to hint at the actual fact."

Miss Emma C. Shipman, of Boston, saw Mrs. Eddy for the first time on May 26, 1895, when the latter delivered her first address in the original building of The Mother Church. "I had looked forward with much eagerness to hearing Mrs. Eddy speak," writes Miss Shipman, "and had pictured her in looks and manner as possibly akin to Julia Ward Howe and Mary A. Livermore, whom I had heard lecture. Instead, there was this great contrast,—one almost lost sight of the personality in drinking in her words. The other two had what one might call big personalities, but

Mrs. Eddy was like a transparency for God to shine through."

Afterward, Miss Shipman had a number of interviews with Mrs. Eddy, and was in her last class. Of this experience, Miss Shipman has written in part as follows: "When Mrs. Eddy came into the class, I experienced the feeling I always had on seeing her, of the greatness of the truth she taught and the self-effacement of the teacher.

"Mrs. Eddy talked much on what love is and the need of more love in our healing work. She said in substance: I want you to think of God as Father, Mother, Shepherd; as the Father who sustains, maintains, supports, and cares for man; as the Mother who takes the little babe to her breast with ineffable tenderness; as the Shepherd who watches over the sheep, seeks the lost lamb, and when the little lamb strays again, goes after it no matter how often it strays, and brings it back, until at last it grows to be a sheep and knows its master's voice, and follows Him. Think of the changeless nature of the Shepherd! You must get a more tender sense of the fatherliness of God. Your God is your Life."

Of Mrs. Eddy's ability and fitness to be the chief teacher of Christian Science she furnished a notable proof in the 1880's, when the public seemed to be in danger of accepting what was then propagated as "mental science" or mind cure instead of Christian Science. Indeed, this propaganda persuaded more than a few avowed Christian

Scientists to prefer a teaching that was mental in some sense but was not purely spiritual. The situation was like the one related in John 6:63–66. When the Master declared, "It is the spirit that quickeneth; the flesh profiteth nothing," a purely spiritual teaching, "many of his disciples went back, and walked no more with him."

Mrs. Eddy faced the danger in question firmly and resourcefully. In particular, she formulated and executed plans to provide more authorized teachers, and she did a great deal of writing, not in the least degree to modify Christian Science, but to make it more widely known and to help the public to comprehend its Principle and its purely spiritual practice. For instance, the following statement in *Retrospection and Introspection* (57:15) can be traced to a pamphlet by Mrs. Eddy which was issued at that time: "Man shines by borrowed light. He reflects God as his Mind, and this reflection is substance,—the substance of good."

PART TWO

ORGANIZATION

CHAPTER XVI

MRS. EDDY AS LEADER

BEFORE she discovered Christian Science, Mary Baker Eddy was not prepared by experience or training to institute a cause or lead a movement of such importance as her great discovery. In certain respects, however, her previous education and experience aided her as the Leader of the Christian Science movement. In particular, she was prepared to speak and write; she had spoken and written frequently on civic and ethical topics, such as the abolition of Negro slavery. Naturally, this experience and training helped her to choose the best means for propagating her religion, and helped her to develop the most effective speaking and writing for this purpose. On the whole, however, Mrs. Eddy's leadership was chiefly inspirational. The discovery itself enabled her to develop an effective and steadfast dependence on divine Mind for necessary guidance and wisdom. Throughout her leadership, it was most characteristic of Mrs. Eddy "to wait on divine Love." [1]

Not only did Mrs. Eddy learn to depend implicitly on God for discernment and direction throughout her leader-

---

[1] *Message to The Mother Church for 1902,* p. 2.

ship of the Christian Science movement, but she also learned to study the lessons of experience in a scientific way. Her attitude toward these subjects could be illustrated by many excerpts from her letters. When writing to The Christian Science Board of Directors in 1895 she said, "And from long *tests* I know that He will show me the way that is just, and then I will follow it." And when writing to the Directors in 1908 she expressed her thought in these few words: "Be wise from inspiration and experience."

Mrs. Eddy got at least an effective glimpse of what she afterward named Christian Science at Lynn in February of 1866. She gained a distinct step toward complete discovery in the latter part of that year. She attained to further stages of progress during the next three years. The discovery of Christian Science continued to develop in her consciousness, the first edition of her principal work being completed in 1875. Naturally, her progress in the comprehension of such a subject did not end then. She has spoken to this effect in her autobiography, *Retrospection and Introspection*, pages 24–28, and in her principal work, *Science and Health with Key to the Scriptures*, ix: 20–2; 109:11; 361:21. If the culminating of her expression can be traced to a particular time, it may be marked by her revision of *Science and Health* in 1901 and her *Messages to The Mother Church* for 1901 and 1902. Afterwards she did less writing, but did it just as well.

From the beginning of her discovery, Mrs. Eddy regarded it unselfishly for its import to all mankind. She regarded it as conveying the highest consequences to all people, and she never lost this point of view. Even while Christian Science was a new subject to her, she sought opportunities to communicate her discovery and to demonstrate its practical value. Soon, she had to choose between living with one of her sisters in New Hampshire, her husband, Dr. Patterson, having deserted her, and continuing to propagate her newly discovered Science. Even though Mrs. Eddy effected a wonderful healing for her niece, Ellen Pilsbury, in 1867, this did not move her sisters to offer her a home unless she would stop disseminating her good news. At about the same time, affluent friends in Lynn offered her a home, but she preferred the more humble environments of Massachusetts villages in which to prepare for her lifework.

During the three and a half years from November of 1866 to May of 1870, Mrs. Eddy lived at Avon, then called East Stoughton, at Taunton, at Amesbury, at Stoughton, and again at Amesbury. During the same period, she also visited at Lynn, at Manchester, New Hampshire, and at Tilton, New Hampshire. During these years, she continued her search for the Science of Mind, she endeavored to formulate her mission, she did some important healing, she taught a few pupils, and she clarified her thought by extensive writing. Instances of the healing that she did during these years are related on page 242 of *Miscellaneous Writings*, on page 54 of *Pulpit and Press*, on pages 40 and 41 of *Retrospection and Introspection*, and on page 105 of *The First Church of Christ, Scientist, and Miscellany*. Other instances from that time are recorded in the files of The Mother Church. The writing that she did then is mentioned on page ix of the Preface to *Science and Health*, on page 27 of *Retrospection and Introspection*, and on page 114 of *Miscellany*.

In 1870, Mrs. Eddy returned to Lynn, where had occurred, as she once wrote, "the re-birth of an idea which vibrates in unison with the divine order." Lynn then had 28,000 inhabitants, of whom 23,000 were native Americans. There, in 1870, she copyrighted her first pamphlet, a manuscript of 5,300 words entitled *The Science of Man*. There, in 1872, she issued her first or next public statement of Christian Science, then called Moral Science. There, in 1875, she completed the first edition of her principal work, then entitled *Science and Health*. There, in 1876, she gave the Christian Science movement its first organization, the Christian Scientist Association. From there, in 1879, she founded the Christian Science Church, the Church of Christ, Scientist, in Boston. At and from Lynn, from 1870 to 1882, she also carried on other methodical seed-sowing and did protective watching; from all of which activities permanent and progressive results have ensued to the present time.

Mrs. Eddy as Leader

A description of Mrs. Eddy as she was from 1870 to 1882 has been left by one of her early pupils, Samuel Putnam Bancroft, who saw her frequently during this time. The following description is abridged and combined from different places in his reminiscences. "Although her resources were meager, she was always neatly and carefully dressed. Her manner was always ladylike and self-possessed, even on the most trying occasions. When in conversation, the animation she displayed added much to her attractiveness. It was the animation of conviction, not of excitement or agitation. She showed no self-consciousness, either in classroom or upon the platform; rather, self-forgetfulness. . . . Although she was writing, teaching and preaching, and occasionally treating some severe case beyond a student's ability to reach, her physical and mental vigor seemed to be augmented rather than depleted. . . . At all times she seemed conscious of a wisdom beyond her own, which she could only attain by continued effort. . . . At the time I knew her, Mrs. Eddy had apparently but one purpose in life, and that was to benefit mankind."

Lynn is only fourteen miles from Boston, and until 1882 Mrs. Eddy divided her activities between these places. Then she settled in Boston. By 1875 or 1876, she had begun to be known to the public of this vicinity as the Discoverer of a Science based on the Bible which healed the sick, as a demonstrator of this Science, as a teacher of it whose students also could heal, as the author of a book containing a statement of her teaching, and as an effective and interesting speaker on the subject to which she devoted her life. Before moving to Boston, she had delivered many lectures and sermons to many different audiences in Boston and its suburbs, to do which she had developed opportunities of extraordinary variety. For instance, beginning in 1878 she preached in a Baptist church in Boston a series of sermons which brought forth excellent results.[1] Early in the 1880's, therefore, Mrs. Eddy had gained a creditable position in public thought. Both she and her teaching had become favorably known to many intelligent people throughout New England. And by 1885 or so, different degrees of this recognition had extended to other parts of the United States as well as to a part of Canada.

The aid given to Mrs. Eddy by particular persons in the early history of Christian Science cannot be more than mentioned here. There were, of course, a considerable number of persons who helped her in different ways during the early part of her great work. Not all of them proved to be stable as Christian Scientists, but others did, and some of them rendered services that were indispensable, especially healing. Besides the impressive healing done by Mrs. Eddy before other duties excluded her from this practice, other practitioners did creditable work; and from the middle of the 1880's their number increased

---

[1] See pages 15 and 16 of *Retrospection and Introspection.*

steadily. So, in a few more years Christian Science needed a new organization—one adapted to its enlarged scope and its future prospects.

In the latter part of the 1880's, there were three organizations besides the Massachusetts Metaphysical College that represented Christian Science in more than a local way. They were the Christian Scientist Association, formed in 1876, the Church of Christ, Scientist, formed in 1879, and the National Christian Scientist Association, formed in 1886. These three institutions are described in later chapters. Each of them had its inception in an immediate need, and each had its own purposes. Although each of these organizations had its own members, membership in one of them did not preclude membership in the others. Members of the Christian Scientist Association could belong to either or both of the other organizations. Any Christian Scientist could belong to the Church, and all Christian Science teachers and their pupils were eligible for membership in the National Christian Scientist Association. Each of these organizations also had its own officers elected by its members; but, in effect, Mrs. Eddy was the chief officer for each of them as the Discoverer and Founder of Christian Science and the Leader of its movement.

From before 1889, Mrs. Eddy planned to simplify and unify the Christian Science organization. She began to formulate an organic structure that would supersede all of the above-named institutions and would be closely adapted to the needs of the Christian Science movement, including its future requirements. At about the same time, she also planned to develop officers for the new structure who could be depended on for the most important administrative or executive functions. In 1889, she induced the members of the Church of Christ, Scientist, to abandon its formal organization, and to leave its affairs to be managed by her and its Directors. From this time, also, she endeavored to leave important decisions to the Directors, and to develop their own resourcefulness. As for the Christian Scientist Association and the National Christian Scientist Association, one of them dissolved itself in 1889, while the other curtailed its functions then, and afterwards maintained not much more than a nominal existence.

In 1892, Mrs. Eddy led a reorganization of the Church of Christ, Scientist, from the unorganized body which had existed since 1889, and named her church The Mother Church, The First Church of Christ, Scientist, in Boston, Massachusetts. Furthermore, from then until the last revision of the Church By-Laws, Mrs. Eddy gave a great deal of thought to adapting and developing the form and functions of this Church so that it would be of the utmost value to the Christian Science movement. In fact, the organization that Mrs. Eddy devised for the Christian Science movement, including The Mother Church, its auxiliaries, and its branches, constitutes a most extraor-

dinary achievement. The early Jewish temple and syna-
gogues, or the Christian church at Jerusalem and elsewhere in the first century, could have furnished a partial
precedent, but only in a very general way. Christian
denominations in recent times could have furnished a few
details. In essential respects, however, Mrs. Eddy devised
and evolved the Christian Science organization in an original manner as the result of inspiration and experience.

Among the characteristic features of the Christian Science Church are its two forms of democracy. The government of The Mother Church is "essentially democratic"[1]
while the government of the branch churches is required
to be "distinctly democratic."[2] A Christian Scientist may
be a member of The Mother Church and of a branch
church. A Christian Science Society is like a branch
church; it is or may be the beginning of a branch church.

Considered deeply, democracy in government has a
spiritual basis, the equality of all men as sons of God. The
Master declared the essence of democracy when he said,
"All ye are brethren. . . . One is your Father, which is in
heaven. . . . He that is greatest among you shall be your
servant" (Matthew 23:8–11). The Shorter Oxford Dictionary furnishes the following definition of "democracy":
"In modern use often denoting a social state in which all
have equal rights."

---

1 *Miscellany*, p. 247.
2 *Church Manual*, p. 74.

The government of The Mother Church is democratic in the sense that all of its members have assented to its constitution, and all of them have equal rights. Thus, they have equal rights to prepare for its ministry or service, and equal rights to be considered according to their evident or known fitness for admission to its accredited ministry, for appointment to its offices, and for other employment in its service. The branch churches can be more democratic, because their members constitute more compact bodies, and because their affairs are more adapted to handling by members as distinguished from officers. Personal dictation would be equally foreign to either The Mother Church or its branches.

In the deed of trust dated September 1, 1892, by which Mrs. Eddy founded The Mother Church,[1] she provided for The Christian Science Board of Directors, a board which was to become an executive body of unique scope and value. At first, part of the authority to represent The Mother Church was given to another board or body called First Members. A statement of their functions and of the procedure by which the same were transferred to the Directors in 1901 may be found in a later chapter. Now, the final law of the Christian Science movement on this subject is summed up in these few words: "The business of The Mother Church shall be transacted by its

---

[1] *Church Manual*, pp. 128–135.

Christian Science Board of Directors."[1] This giving of chief responsibility to one board composed of a few persons Mrs. Eddy contemplated before 1901 for several years, and she tested it afterwards for nine years. This constitutional provision has also withstood the tests of the subsequent years.

The teaching that Mrs. Eddy did while she conducted the Massachusetts Metaphysical College can be assigned to her activities as the Leader of the Christian Science movement, and can be regarded as one of the most important parts of her entire work. This teaching continued from 1881 to 1889. After closing the College in 1889, she did not teach again until 1898, when she taught her last class.

As a general rule, Mrs. Eddy's earlier classes were composed of applicants for them, but the class that she taught at Concord in November of 1898 consisted of sixty-five representative Christian Scientists whom she invited for this opportunity. A few of them had applied for her teaching in previous years. Two representatives of the press were also present. As thus constituted, it was the privilege of this class to hear two lessons intended to be of benefit, not only to its members, but also to the Christian Science movement as a whole.[2]

Although Mrs. Eddy lived at Concord, New Hampshire, for almost nineteen years before returning to a

[1] *Church Manual*, p. 27.
[2] See *Miscellany*, pp. 104, 125, 243–244.

suburb of Boston, in 1908, she continued to keep in close contact with Christian Science affairs. The officers of her Church consulted her constantly; they also reported to her frequently by the different modes of communication then in use. Furthermore, she carried on a large correspondence with other Christian Scientists. Indeed, she kept herself generally well informed concerning conditions and events, both in and out of the Christian Science movement, until she passed to another state of consciousness in 1910. During her entire leadership, she considered the major conditions and events of all human life, and acted in view of them; for, as she has said in her autobiography, her motive was "to relieve the sufferings of humanity by a sanitary system that should include all moral and religious reform." [1]

As the Leader of the Christian Science movement, Mrs. Eddy was always disposed to consider suggestions from Christian Scientists, but her mail became too large for her to examine. Afterwards it was sorted by her secretaries, and she saw only the more important letters. Likewise, the number of callers whom she could receive became fewer as the movement grew and as she could leave more responsibility to The Christian Science Board of Directors. Recommendations from this Board she always considered thoughtfully. She also consulted the Directors as occasions occurred. In many instances, however, she decided upon

---

[1] *Retrospection and Introspection*, p. 30.

acts of major importance without consulting anybody. She depended on divine guidance; and when she felt sure that the divine Mind had spoken to her, she did not hesitate. Her attitude was that she had to obey God, even before she knew the reason why.

CHAPTER XVII

THE FIRST ORGANIZATION

CHAPTER XVII

THE FIRST ORGANIZATION

THE Christian Science movement started slowly. Yet, by 1876, ten years after her discovery of Christian Science, Mary Baker Eddy, then Mary Baker Glover, had healed and taught a considerable number of persons. Her students, also, had done some healing. Not all of the beneficiaries had become Christian Scientists; but enough had, so that a movement existed then composed of Mrs. Eddy and her followers. In 1875, a few of them arranged with her for "meetings on the Sabbath of each week" to be conducted by her "as teacher or instructor," which meetings preceded by four years the Church of Christ, Scientist. It can be said, however, that the Christian Science movement was first organized at Lynn, Massachusetts, in 1876, when Mrs. Eddy and almost the same students formed the Christian Scientist Association. [1]

Among Christian Scientists, the word "association" has a particular meaning now which it did not have in 1876. The first Association was not limited to purposes connected with study or teaching; its purposes extended to

---

[1] See *Retrospection and Introspection*, p. 43.

the entire interest in which Christian Scientists were united. As the preamble to the constitution of the Christian Scientist Association declared, it was "the oldest society of the School of Mind-healing, Christian Science." In short, this Association was not only an association of teacher and pupils; it was also an organization for promoting a distinct religion.

The Church of Christ, Scientist, was organized at Boston in 1879, after having been given its inception by the Christian Scientist Association. A motion by Mrs. Eddy at a meeting of the Association and a vote by the fourteen or fifteen other members who were present gave the Church its initiative. It was distinctly and completely organized a few months later.

At first, the Church of Christ, Scientist, did little more than hold Sunday services. After a considerable time, it began to represent the Christian Science movement in a general way. Yet, the Christian Scientist Association continued to do this too. At a meeting of the Association in 1883, Mrs. Eddy said that "the Association should be merged into the Church," but this was not done then; the Association continued its own existence until it was dissolved in the fall of 1889 on Mrs. Eddy's advice and request. From this time, the Christian Scientist Association, now called Christian Scientist Association of the Massachusetts Metaphysical College, ceased to act in its original character; it ceased to represent the Christian Science movement in a general way, and its members continued to meet only as students of the College.

During its thirteen years, the Christian Scientist Association had regular meetings once in two weeks or once in four weeks. Special meetings were held as occasions occurred. Until Mrs. Eddy removed from Lynn to Boston in 1882, nearly half of its meetings were held in her home. The others were held at the homes of other members in near-by towns or in Boston. After Mrs. Eddy became a resident of Boston, all meetings of the Association were held there, at first in her home, later in different chapels and halls.

From its beginning, the Christian Scientist Association consisted chiefly of Mrs. Eddy and persons whom she had taught in a class or less formally. After 1885 the admission of members was explicitly limited to persons who had taken a course of instruction from her. There were, however, a few honorary members and there were visitors. In the first few years, all members were from Massachusetts and adjacent states. Later, the membership extended to more distant localities as the demand for Mrs. Eddy's instruction spread and pupils in her classes became members of the Association. At no time, however, did it include all her students.

After an informal beginning, the Christian Scientist Association adopted a constitution, by-laws, and rules of order, which were amended from time to time. Mrs. Eddy drafted the original provisions and at least most of the amendments, but she always submitted them to the members for discussion and vote. In the few cases when objections were made, Mrs. Eddy made explanations if they were needed, and evinced a willingness to accept amendments and consider objections. This was her attitude, for instance, when one of the members refused to sign the constitution and by-laws because, as he thought, they gave Mrs. Eddy too much power.

As drafted by Mrs. Eddy, the constitution of the Christian Scientist Association included a carefully formulated statement of her discovery: "to wit; that a Divine principle and given rule applicable to every condition of man, and constituting the Divine plan of his salvation from sin, sickness and death exist in the order of Eternal life, Truth, and Love, and that Jesus demonstrated for man's example and his redemption, this holy principle of Divine Science, healing the sick, casting out devils, error, and raising the dead; clearly showing by this Divine understanding and proof, the indivisibility of Science and Christianity." The foregoing quotation is from the constitution as first printed, in which the capitalization and punctuation may have been furnished by the printer.

All meetings of the Christian Scientist Association were conducted in a democratic, though formal, manner. Points or questions were debated; all members were expected to participate in the discussions, and all were expected to vote on every question, unless excused from voting. Mrs. Eddy often presided, and oftener than otherwise she contributed to a meeting by elucidating a point in Christian Science. At different times, also, under the auspices of the Association, she delivered lectures on Christian Science to invited persons or to the public. Thus, the annual report of the secretary dated January 15, 1880, included the following item: "From November 1878 to July 1879, Mrs. Eddy delivered 32 lectures in Boston, holding good audiences."

When the Church of Christ, Scientist, was organized in 1879, most members of the Christian Scientist Association, but not all of them, became members of the Church, and for several years the Association had a parental attitude toward the Church. For instance, on May 26, 1880, the Church asked the Association for the money in its treasury "to help liquidate the Church debt," and the request was granted by unanimous vote. On June 30, 1880, the Association voted to pay the rent of the Church's meeting place for Sunday services four weeks in advance. One of the speakers said that members of the Association who were not members of the Church should feel the duty to help support the Church, "it being all the same cause."

As the Christian Scientist Association promoted the Church of Christ, Scientist, so did the Association promote *The Christian Science Journal* and what afterward became The Christian Science Publishing Society. On January 17, 1883, "the subject of a publication for the good of the

Cause was introduced, and some of the many objects to be gained by such an organ were warmly discussed." A committee was constituted for this purpose, which reported favorably on January 31. On March 1, Mrs. Eddy said, "If I have to give up other work, we will have the paper." The first number of *The Christian Science Journal* was issued the next month. At first the *Journal* did not describe itself as an organ, but later its front cover described the *Journal* as the official organ of the Church and the Association.

Through the Christian Scientist Association, Mrs. Eddy also originated the Committee on Publication and the Reading Room. The first Committee on Publication was constituted on February 4, 1885, and was discontinued on June 12, 1888. The question of establishing a Reading Room began to be discussed in the spring of 1887. Delays ensued from changes of plan, difficulties in finding a feasible location, and a postponement until "more propitious times." Finally, in the fall of 1888, a meeting place for the Association, an office for *The Christian Science Journal*, and a room for a Reading Room were leased and occupied in the Hotel Boylston, at the southeast corner of Boylston and Tremont Streets, Boston, which site was later occupied by the Hotel Touraine. At this time, the Sunday services of the Church of Christ, Scientist, were held in Chickering Hall, two blocks northward on Tremont Street.

The minutes kept by the Christian Scientist Association include many interesting items. Here is one dated August 15, 1878: "It was unanimously voted to defer to Mrs. Eddy the right to decide under what name the students of Christian Science shall appear before the public. The choice lay between 'Christian Scientist' and 'Metaphysician.' After due consideration, Mrs. Eddy fixed upon 'Christian Scientist' as the only name to be used in the future."

At more than a few meetings of this Association, Mrs. Eddy answered questions or gave advice on Christian Science healing. While doing this on January 17, 1883, she related the following incident, probably connected with the second edition of *Science and Health:* "One of the best cures I ever performed was, apparently, under the most adverse circumstances. I had spent one year of incessant toil upon the MSS. of my book, 'Science and Health,' and put it into the hands of a printer for publication, who, I found, had allowed it to be taken from his possession, and I was thus obliged to return, in the sackcloth of disappointment, without it. A student soon called desiring me to assist in a case that was dying. I put on the wedding garments at once and healed the case in twenty minutes."

By 1885, Mrs. Eddy had equipped other Christian Science practitioners, had founded the Church of Christ, Scientist, had enlarged the Christian Science textbook, had started *The Christian Science Journal*, had spread Christian

Hotel Boylston, Boston — Early Home of the Publishing Society

Science beyond its first locality, and had led all who were prepared to follow through enough Red Sea and wilderness, enough halting conditions and reversing circumstances, to demonstrate her dependable leadership. By this time, therefore, Mrs. Eddy had become actually and evidently the Discoverer and Founder of Christian Science and the Leader of the Christian Science movement.

One of the conditions which confronted Mrs. Eddy early in the 1880's was the danger that Christian Science could not be extended widely, but would be confined to the locality of its origin. For it to fulfill its mission, she had to discern and adopt such means and methods for sowing "the good seed" as would correspond to the Master's pronouncement, "The field is the world" (Matt. 13:38). The difficulties of this task would have dismayed anyone who was less confident of divine calling and guidance. As yet the Christian Scientist Association organized in 1876 and the Church of Christ, Scientist, organized in 1879 had only a few members living more than a hundred miles from Boston. Soon, however, Mrs. Eddy's efforts, including her healing works, together with the measures just stated, and the healing which they promoted, brought forth greater results. Thus, the classes in her College began to be larger, and she taught one class in Chicago. By 1885, therefore, the Christian Science movement can be said to have broken through its earlier confines, and to have begun to occupy its larger and unlimited field.

Another condition that confronted Mrs. Eddy early in the 1880's was the danger that Christian Science would be confused with and hidden by the many isms then in vogue which were mental but not spiritual—which were based on the so-called human will, not on the divine Mind. Often named or misnamed "Mental Science" and "Mind Cure," they could have been called "Legion," for they were many (Mark 5:9). To avert this danger as well as to advance the Christian Science movement in a normal way, Mrs. Eddy formulated plans for proclaiming the unique nature of this Science and for extending the knowledge of it by more class teaching. These plans she put into execution immediately.

Until August of 1884, Mrs. Eddy was the only authorized teacher of Christian Science. In that month, by teaching a Normal class in the Massachusetts Metaphysical College she prepared its ten members to be teachers. The first of their cards as teachers appeared in the *Journal* for November 1, 1884. Then from 1885 to 1888, she taught other Normal classes which added to the number of authorized teachers, and she instructed them, "Teach all the students you can get (ready and fit for being taught)." This procedure gave a strong impetus to the movement, for the new teachers became active as missionaries, and opened their classes to inquirers, some of whom may not have had much more than an incipient interest in Christian Science.

The First Organization

At this critical time, Mrs. Eddy also did a large amount of writing. In 1885, she issued a pamphlet entitled *Historical Sketch of Metaphysical Healing*. In 1886 and 1888, she revised this pamphlet as *Mind-Healing: Historical Sketch* and *Historical Sketch of Christian Science Mind-Healing*. Each edition of this pamphlet was distributed widely. In 1887, she issued a book entitled *Christian Science: No and Yes*, and another pamphlet entitled *Rudiments and Rules of Divine Science*. In 1887, she issued another book entitled *Unity of Good and Unreality of Evil*. In 1891, the first of these pamphlets became parts of another book by Mrs. Eddy entitled *Retrospection and Introspection*. In the same year, she enlarged the other pamphlet just mentioned, and made it a book entitled *Rudimental Divine Science*. Further, in 1891 she revised *Christian Science: No and Yes* and named it *No and Yes;* also, she revised *Unity of Good and Unreality of Evil* and named it *Unity of Good*. Although these new publications were not limited to any particular need or purpose, they were particularly effective for the purpose of distinguishing Christian Science from other teachings and emphasizing its essence as not only mental but also spiritual.

The major problem that confronted Mrs. Eddy in the late 1880's and the early 1890's was the need for an appropriate and adequate agency to be the central administrative and executive body of the Christian Science movement. Naturally, a religion should be represented by a church; and neither the Christian Scientist Association nor the National Christian Scientist Association was a church. Evidently, therefore, the Church of Christ, Scientist, was more adaptable to the need; its possibilities were sufficient; and it was already known as The Mother Church. Yet, as the Church existed in 1889, its constitution was not adapted to the functions necessary to be exercised in behalf of the entire movement. Furthermore, the Church's record for ten years had shown that the members as a whole were not prepared to assume any such responsibility.

In this situation, Mrs. Eddy recommended a course of action which resulted, after nearly three years, in what is now The Mother Church. The Church of Christ, Scientist, abandoned its formal organization and procedures, but retained its continuity and name. From December 2, 1889, to September 23, 1892, the Church carried on its former work as an informal society, its affairs being managed by a Board of Directors. These Directors consisted of those who were in office when the Church was dissolved in 1889 and others whom they elected. The main reasons for this long interval were instances of dissent and discord among a minority of the members and a failure of the members as a whole to develop the stability and wisdom required for conducting the affairs of what was to be The Mother Church. In 1892, however, Mrs. Eddy and chosen members of this informal society, reorganized it, thus forming The First Church of Christ, Scientist, as she has related on page 18 of the *Church Manual of The First Church of Christ, Scientist,* and on page 20 of *Pulpit and Press.* Later, the government of The Mother Church was reconstituted and simplified by abolishing the office of First Members.

In a letter to a student dated December 20, 1889, Mrs. Eddy said, "Twenty-three years have shown that everything that I have done has had back of it a higher wisdom than mine." The period indicated by these words began with her discovery of Christian Science; and it can be added that Mrs. Eddy's receiving of God-given wisdom neither ended nor abated at the date of her letter.

CHAPTER XVIII

INSTANCES OF OUTGROWN PROCEDURE

FROM 1876, Mrs. Eddy and part of her students—presumably all whom she expected to become teachers—constituted the Christian Scientist Association or were its principal members. In 1884, when she first began to commission her most promising students as teachers, they, in turn, began to form associations consisting of themselves and their pupils.

In 1886, at Mrs. Eddy's suggestion, there was formed the National Christian Scientist Association, of which teachers and their pupils could become members. It was formed, as she has said, "To meet the broader wants of humanity, and provide folds for the sheep that were without shepherds." [1] The organizers of the new Association voted as follows: "The purpose or object of this National Association is to give students' students an equal footing with others in Christian Science and to promote unity and brotherly love. Charters will be granted by this National Association to the minor Associations."

As she has said, [2] Mrs. Eddy wrote the constitution of

---

[1] *Retrospection and Introspection*, p. 52.
[2] *Miscellaneous Writings*, p. 382.

the National Christian Scientist Association, which declared its powers in these words: "This National Christian Scientist Association has exclusive jurisdiction in granting charters. No Students Christian Scientist Association can be formed or continue to exist without its sanction. It possesses the sole right and power of granting charters; of suspending or taking away charters for proper cause; of receiving appeals and redressing grievances arising in Students Christian Scientist Associations; of originating and regulating the means of its own support; and of doing all other acts conducive to the interest of the Order." In the last clause of the foregoing provision, "the Order" meant Christian Science or the Christian Science movement. The entire provision, therefore, assumed or conferred power to supervise teaching and power to do anything else that would contribute to the development of Christian Science.

In its actual working, most of what the National Christian Scientist Association did from 1886 to 1890 was to adopt and amend its constitution, admit members, grant charters, and listen to addresses and discussions. During the latter part of this period, it also endeavored to promote the organization of churches and dispensaries. And from 1889 to 1897, it held *The Christian Science Journal* as its official organ, by gift from Mrs. Eddy, but this holding did not include editing or management. In fact, the National Association's existence after its annual meeting in 1890 was not much more than nominal.

Although named "National," the National Christian Scientist Association was not limited to the United States; it had members from Canada, and could have had members from other countries. The meetings to organize it were held in Boston and New York in 1886; its later meetings for particular purposes were held in Boston; its annual meetings were held in Boston in 1886 and 1887, Chicago in 1888, Cleveland in 1889, and New York in 1890.

The second annual meeting of the National Christian Scientist Association occurred in Boston on April 13 and 14, 1887. The notice of it invited all teachers and their pupils, and informed them that Mrs. Eddy would address the meeting. Besides the notice in *The Christian Science Journal*, Mrs. Eddy sent letters to many of the teachers, urging them to be present, and saying that she had for them "a message from God." One hundred and forty-six persons from fifteen states attended the first session in Meionaon Hall, Tremont Temple Building. The number who heard Mrs. Eddy's address at a later session was not recorded, nor was her address either written or adequately reported. This convention was an important occasion, but the proceedings indicated that the Association as such was not adapted to executive functions.

The apex of the National Christian Scientist Association was attained at and by its Chicago convention in 1888. Mrs. Eddy had given a great impetus to Christian Science in the central and western parts of the United States by a month of work there in 1884, during which she taught a class of representative students. For the meeting of 1888 she issued an urgent call in *The Christian Science Journal* (Vol. VI, p. 154), which can be read now on pages 134-135 of *Miscellaneous Writings*. As originally published, this call was addressed to Christian Scientists, and ended with the words, "Mrs. Eddy will herself attend the convention." To the many who responded, she delivered the memorable address on "Science and the Senses," of which the substance was printed in the *Journal* (Vol. VI, p. 217) and is preserved in revised form on pages 98–106 of *Miscellaneous Writings*. Although not previously reduced to writing, this address can be rated as one of Mrs. Eddy's most notable utterances. As was said by the Editor of *The Christian Science Journal* (Vol. VI, p. 206), "From the depths of her personal experience, and out [of] a heart yearning to bestow its priceless treasures upon those who listened, the revered Teacher, Mrs. Eddy, spoke."

Mrs. Eddy has left an account of her Chicago address and reception in *The Christian Science Journal* (Vol. VI, p. 212) and in revised form on pages 275–276 of *Miscellaneous Writings*. So has the National Christian Scientist Association in its record, as follows: "At 10 a. m. our Teacher spoke to an immense audience in Central Music Hall; which long before the doors were thrown open was packed with people anxious to see her and hear her speak. At the close, many affecting scenes took place by those who were unable to take her by the hand. In the evening, a grand reception was accorded her, but only for a short time did she remain among them." The Chicago convention was attended by perhaps one thousand Christian Scientists, while Mrs. Eddy's address was heard by between three thousand and four thousand people.

Although Mrs. Eddy formulated the National Christian Scientist Association, became its President, and at first supervised its work, she endeavored to limit her part in its management and to develop other executives. To its meeting at Cleveland, in 1889, she sent her resignation as President. To its meeting in New York, the next year, she sent a communication which was printed in the *Journal* (Vol. VIII, p. 139) and is preserved in revised form on pages 137–139 of *Miscellaneous Writings*, which resulted in the discontinuance of its active work. Thereafter, the associations of pupils continued by themselves. The National Association did not meet again, except that the Christian Science Convention held at Chicago in 1893, as part of the world's Parliament of Religions, was regarded as an adjourned meeting of this Association.

Briefly and chiefly, the National Christian Scientist Association can be described as a plan to improve the service rendered by teachers, to help care for pupils, and to promote unity in the thought of Christian Scientists. Even more comprehensively can this description be applied to another plan including these purposes, called the

General Association of Teachers. Instituted in 1903, by an Article in the *Manual* of The Mother Church, it lasted until 1908, when it was dissolved by the repeal of its authorization in the Church By-Laws. The original provision for a General Association of Teachers was Article XXXIII in the twenty-ninth edition of the *Manual* (1903). As amended and developed, this provision became Article XXXIII in the forty-ninth edition (1905), and it appeared last in the seventy-second edition (1908).

Besides the General Association of Teachers established in the United States, there were Associations of Teachers in Canada, England, Scotland, and Germany. Each body consisted of loyal Christian Scientists having a degree, C. S. B. or C. S. D., from the Massachusetts Metaphysical College or the Christian Science Board of Education. The General Association met in Boston in 1903, in Chicago in 1904, and in New York in 1905. It did not meet after 1905, because the original provision for annual meetings was changed to biennial and to triennial meetings, and all of the Associations were dissolved before the date for another meeting. The minor Associations met in their respective countries, except that by permission from Mrs. Eddy the Canadian teachers attended the General Association's meeting in New York in 1905.

The arrangements for the first meeting of the General Association of Teachers, including the program, were made by The Christian Science Board of Directors and the teacher of the Board of Education, Mr. Edward A. Kimball. After the first meeting, the General Association was given an Executive Board, which arranged for the second and third meetings. To the General Association at its first meeting, Mrs. Eddy sent a letter including these words: "You have convened only to convince yourselves of this grand verity: namely, the unity in Christian Science. Cherish steadfastly this fact. Adhere to the teachings of the Bible, Science and Health, and our Manual, and you will obey the law and gospel." The entire letter may be read on pages 251–252 of *The First Church of Christ, Scientist, and Miscellany*. The foregoing words are quoted here because they indicate the principal subjects which were discussed at all meetings of the General Association.

The program for each meeting of the General Association of Teachers was arranged in advance, and consisted mainly of carefully prepared papers by a considerable number of members. After the first meeting, the *Manual* specified *"unity of action,* strict conformity to the Mother Church By-Laws, and to the contents of the chapter on Teaching Christian Science" in *Science and Health* as "the main topics for discussion." As amended to institute the Association the *Manual* provided that "the rule of uniformity in the teaching and practice of Christian Science shall be strictly adhered to by both teacher and pupil." Therefore, the papers read covered almost every phase of the subjects indicated by these quotations.

[178]

After the first meeting of the General Association of Teachers, the *Manual* also contained the following provision: "A two-thirds vote of the Executive Board shall elect or dismiss a member from the General Association of Teachers, and if dismissed, this member shall no longer be regarded as a teacher of Christian Science." In actual working, however, neither the General Association nor its Executive Board attempted to administer discipline or adjudge personal issues.

Doubtless the National Christian Scientist Association and the General Association of Teachers did a great deal of good. Each of these agencies was required by the conditions of its time. Yet, from what they accomplished, or failed to accomplish, the conclusion can be drawn reasonably that the most dependable agencies for maintaining uniformity in the teaching and practice of Christian Science are the Board of Directors and the Board of Education of The Mother Church, acting under the final provisions of the *Church Manual* (Article XII; Article XXV, Section 9; Articles XXVI–XXX). A comprehensive review of Mrs. Eddy's entire work discloses that she acquired wisdom by direct impartations from the infinite source and by inductions from experience.

CHAPTER XIX

OTHER DISCONTINUED MODES

AT the end of 1886, the Christian Science movement was represented by a complexity of organizations. There were the Church of Christ, Scientist, in Boston, and a few churches at other places. There were also the Christian Scientist Association of the Massachusetts Metaphysical College, the National Christian Scientist Association, and minor Christian Scientist Associations composed of teachers and their pupils.

In January, 1887, a group of Christian Scientists, members of the Church of Christ, Scientist, in Boston, instituted a further organized work named "Free Dispensary of Christian Science Healing." They declared their purpose in these words: "We, the undersigned, hereby associate ourselves for the purpose of promoting the spiritual and physical welfare of the worldly poor; to teach them better health and morals, and to show them by practical methods how to improve their condition and live the truest lives." For this purpose, rooms were engaged at 3 Boylston Place, Boston, just off Boylston Street between Park Square and Tremont Street.

Although the work thus begun in 1887 was carried on

by members of the Church of Christ, Scientist, they appear to have acted independently. Their activity was not mentioned in *The Christian Science Journal* until March, 1889 (Vol. VI, p. 642), not long before it was discontinued because of a similar work organized directly under the auspices of the Church of Christ, Scientist. In June, 1889, the "Free Dispensary of Christian Science Healing" reported in the *Journal* (Vol. VII, p. 154) that between two hundred and three hundred persons had been treated, that "the results have been most cheering," and that the evening "talks" in the Dispensary's hall had been attended by audiences of from seventy to over one hundred people.

At its meeting in March, 1889, the Christian Scientist Association of the Massachusetts Metaphysical College discussed the dispensary work favorably (*Journal*, Vol. VII, p. 145). Then in June, the National Christian Scientist Association also discussed it favorably, but adopted the following resolution: "That in all places where Churches of Christ (Scientist) or Christian Scientist Associations exist, all dispensary work should be conducted under the auspices of such church or association, and that its conduct in such cases independently of such organizations, be discountenanced" (*Journal*, Vol. VII, p. 180). Apparently, the "Free Dispensary of Christian Science Healing" was discontinued pursuant to this resolution.

On Easter Sunday, April 21, 1889, Mrs. Eddy announced that the Church of Christ, Scientist, would have a "Christian Science Dispensary." Accordingly an association for this purpose was organized on May 17, of which she became the Honorary President. This Association opened "Christian Science Rooms and Dispensary" at 7 Temple Street, Boston, in May, 1889. At that time, this location, near Bowdoin Square, was about as convenient as could be found.

The Christian Science Dispensary Association divided its activities into three parts. In certain rooms, meetings open to the public were held every Wednesday and Sunday evening "for addresses, conversation, and inquiry about Christian Science healing;" also, Bible classes every Sunday afternoon "for instruction in the spiritual sense of the Scriptures." Other rooms were open daily from 9 a.m. to 9 p.m. "for the reception and treatment of patients by Christian Science Mind-healing." This activity further included "conversations on Christian Science every evening from 7.30 to 9.30;" also, Christian Science literature free or on sale. The other part of the Association's work was the sending of visitors from house to house "for the purpose of talking Christian Science to the inmates and inviting them to come to the Bible class and other meetings . . . and for physical healing." These visitors carried Christian Science literature, to be given away or sold, according to the circumstances. The healing was offered gratuitously, but applicants for healing were expected to pay something if they could, and contributions for the entire work were solicited. As fast as persons became sufficiently interested, they were to be brought to the church's services and its Sunday school. At this time (1889), the Sunday services and the Sunday school were held at different hours, and pupils of all ages could attend the Sunday school.

The Christian Science Dispensary Association kept a record of its work, and an item in the *Journal* (Vol. VII, p. 194) shows that it was obliged to ask Christian Scientists to stay away from its Sunday and Wednesday meetings because the available room was needed for inquirers. The Dispensary Association continued its work until 1894, when it was stopped by Mrs. Eddy's decision, except to the extent that the dispensary work was continued by the Reading Room of that time. There were dispensaries at other places than Boston—about thirty—of which the earliest were in New York City and Cleveland, Ohio. These dispensaries were not identical in plan or scope, but in different degrees they followed one or the other of the Boston dispensaries as a model.

Presumably, the house-to-house mode of introducing Christian Science was discontinued because it was only adapted to a new subject and because more dignified modes became more suitable for the Christian Science movement. Afterward, however, The Mother Church employed missionaries in other ways. For a period, including 1895, it had a Board of Missionaries "to supply sections that have no healers or teachers in Christian Science."[1] Then, from 1897 to 1906, the *Church Manual* (sixth edition, Article IX, to fifty-third edition, Article XXXVI) provided for the election of "experienced, competent Christian Scientists for missionary work." They were to go wherever the Board of Directors sent them, and were "to do whatever is needed and required of them,—be it to fill a vacancy, or to spread the gospel of Christian Science, or to correctly propagate this Science in whatever locality it is most needed."

The Christian Science Board of Lectureship dates from 1898; hence, from then until 1906 The Mother Church had both lecturers and missionaries. And the foregoing statement of their duties shows that the missionaries could deliver lectures. Furthermore, in 1908, as well as now, the lecturers when called on by the Board of Directors could speak "at such places and at such times as the cause of Christian Science demands."[2] It was the Board of Directors which kept the functions of the lecturers and of the missionaries from conflicting. To an extent, therefore, the lecturers can be said to have succeeded the missionaries.

Another discontinued mode of action found in the history of the Christian Science movement was the participation by "First Members" in the government of The

---

1 *Church Manual*, first edition, Article IX.
2 *Church Manual*, final edition, Article XXXII, Section 1 as compared with Section 2.

Mother Church. The government of its predecessor, the Church of Christ, Scientist, organized in 1879, was congregational. Its members had the right to elect its officers, supervise their work, and act generally as voting members. The Mother Church, The First Church of Christ, Scientist, in Boston, Massachusetts, organized in 1892, followed a different plan. As planned by Mrs. Eddy and duly organized, its government under her jurisdiction was placed in its Board of Directors, and a number of members who were designated as First Members. The First Members only were to transact church business at meetings for this purpose; they were to meet four times a year regularly; a special meeting could be called at any time; and seven First Members would constitute a quorum.[1] The number of First Members was from twelve to one hundred at different times.

In the beginning of The Mother Church, the First Members had many functions. They elected new members and elected other First Members as the number of them was increased or as vacancies occurred. It was the First Members, also, who could expel members and could adopt or change the Church By-Laws as Mrs. Eddy proposed By-Laws or changes in them. It was the First Members, too, who could put a teacher on probation and restore him to good standing. At different times, they had other functions of an executive nature. In particular, from 1898 to

---

[1] *Church Manual,* first edition, Articles I–III.

1901 the power to remove Trustees of The Christian Science Publishing Society was vested in the Directors of The Mother Church and the First Members acting together. In 1901, Mrs. Eddy proposed and the First Members adopted the following By-Law: "The business of The Mother Church hitherto transacted by the First Members shall be done by its Christian Science Board of Directors."[1] In 1919, dissenting Trustees of the Publishing Society contested this transfer and unification, but it was completely upheld by the Supreme Judicial Court of Massachusetts. In 1903, the First Members became "Executive Members," but after 1901 until it was abolished in 1908 their position had no function or use except that only First or Executive Members were eligible for election as Readers or as President.

Christian Science had to have a Discoverer and a Founder. Mary Baker Eddy filled and fulfilled both of these offices. In neither of them was her work completed instantly. In both it developed in accordance with her precept, "Spiritual ideas unfold as we advance."[2] In the end, however, she completed both our textbook and our *Church Manual*, of which she once spoke as follows,[3] "Adhere to the teachings of the Bible, Science and Health, and our Manual, and you will obey the law and gospel."

---

[1] *Church Manual*, twentieth edition, Article VI; and see final edition, Article I, Section 6.
[2] *Science and Health*, p. 361.
[3] *Miscellany*, pp. 251–252.

CHAPTER XX

OTHER INTERESTING EPISODES

MANY Christian Scientists know that, from the beginning of the Church of Christ, Scientist, in 1879, a discourse by Mrs. Eddy was the major part of its Sunday service. Her speaking was usually announced as an address, but sometimes as a Bible lesson or a sermon. It is not so well known that when this Church began to hold midweek meetings, they included a lecture by Mrs. Eddy or by one of her students. Thus, the Church notice in the first issue of the *Journal of Christian Science*, April 14, 1883, announced an address by the Pastor, Mary B. G. Eddy, every Sunday at 3 p.m., and a lecture, free to all, every Thursday evening at 7.30 p.m. "The lecture is followed by discussion, and practical explanation of Christian Science." Later notices read that Mrs. Eddy would speak from time to time, assisted by her students. The time for the midweek meeting, usually spoken of as the lecture, was changed in the latter part of 1883 from Thursday evening to Friday evening. Its program was changed in 1889 to "an address, relation of experiences, and discussions on inquiries from the audience." [1]

---

[1] *Journal*, Vol. VII, p. 100.

At this time, Mrs. Eddy was still Pastor of the Church of Christ, Scientist, but she had an assistant who did nearly all of the public speaking.

The Friday Evening Meetings of the Church of Christ, Scientist, and of The Mother Church continued until June, 1898, when Mrs. Eddy changed the time to Wednesday evening. [1] She gave the midweek meeting its present name, "Wednesday Evening Meeting," in September, 1898. [2] The Friday Evening Meeting had become an experience or testimonial meeting, but she now announced that the Wednesday Evening Meeting would be "a meeting of interest on subjects pertaining to Christian Science, as well as personal experience;" also, that "a member of the Board of Lectureship may lecture at these meetings as often as once in three months." The present program for these meetings dates from 1900.

For a time, contributions were collected at the Friday Evening Meetings of The Mother Church. Contributions at these meetings were discontinued in October, 1895, pursuant to the letter from Mrs. Eddy which is on pages 148–149 of *Miscellaneous Writings*. Since then, no ordinary collection has been taken at a midweek meeting of The Mother Church. In 1906, however, Mrs. Eddy said that contributions for a particular donation, on account of the San Francisco fire, could be collected, either on

---

1 *Journal*, Vol. XVI, p. 167.
2 *Journal*, Vol. XVI, pp. 459, 590.

Wednesday evening or on Sunday. And in 1909, she approved the collections for the local charity fund of The Mother Church which have been taken twice a year since then.

The first Christian Science Sunday School was conducted in 1881 by Asa G. Eddy. Although conducted for the Church of Christ, Scientist, it is not mentioned in the Church's minutes. Probably it was informal, and did not last long. Probably, also, it was for adults, rather than for children. Mrs. Eddy preserved the history of this inception of our Sunday School by mentioning it in certain editions of *Science and Health* and on page 42 of *Retrospection and Introspection*.

In the fall of 1883, the Church of Christ, Scientist, decided to have a Sunday School, and arranged to hold it before the Sunday service. Yet, the execution of this plan was postponed. Instead, for a time, the main feature of the Sunday service was to be a Bible lesson, rather than a sermon.

The Sunday School of the Church of Christ, Scientist, was actually formed on October 25, 1885.[1] There were elected a Superintendent, an Assistant Superintendent, a Secretary, a Treasurer, a Chorister, and a Committee on Music, besides six teachers. After the Church service on the next Sunday, the Superintendent of the Sunday School invited all who desired to become members, which invita-

---

[1] *Miscellany*, p. 55.

tion was accepted by "seventy adults and children." The number of children, as compared with the number of older persons, was not recorded, but a few Sundays later, when the Sunday School numbered 102 pupils besides eleven officers and teachers, a visitor noted that "those present were mostly adults."[1] This Sunday School met at a different time from the Church service, either before or after; and it continued, subject to interruptions and vacations, until 1892, when the present Church, The First Church of Christ, Scientist, in Boston, Massachusetts, was organized. The Sunday School of The Mother Church for children has been held at the same time as its morning service continuously since 1906 and most of the time since 1896.

In contrast with our present usages, an early episode that seems odd or strange was a christening of children by the Pastor of the Church of Christ, Scientist. On February 26, 1888, in Chickering Hall, Mrs. Eddy christened twenty-nine children. Their names, plus the fact that she christened them at this time and place, were entered in the Church record. As described in *The Christian Science Journal* for March, 1888 (Vol. V, p. 629), the christening service took the place of the regular Sunday service, and included an address on names and baptism by the Pastor. The christening itself was described in these words: "Raising her hands over each in turn, she then

---

[1] *Journal,* Vol. III, p. 185.

repeated the name, and very slowly and emphatically pronounced this blessing: 'May the baptism of Christ with the Holy Spirit cleanse you from sin, sickness, and death.' " The rite did not include the use of water. Three of the children were Mrs. Eddy's grandchildren. This christening appears to have been both the first and the last in the Church of Christ, Scientist.

Mrs. Eddy showed her love for children in many ways. In *The Christian Science Journal* for April, 1895 (Vol. XIII, p. 2), she made the following announcement: "On the first Sunday of each month a sermon shall be preached to the children, from selections taken from the Scriptures and Science and Health, specially adapted to the occasion, and read after the manner of the Sunday service." The first of these children's services occurred in Boston on April 14, 1895. As reported in the next issue of the *Journal* (Vol. XIII, pp. 47–48), the main features of the service were the children's sermon and music by a choir from First Church of Christ, Scientist, of New York City. In the *Journal* for the next month (Vol. XIII, p. 100), there was an announcement that the children's service would occur once in four months, and the date of the next one was given, but this plan appears to have been abandoned before this date.

In the October number of the *Journal* (Vol. XIII, p. 268), there was a notice from Mrs. Eddy headed, "What We Can Do for the Children," in which she notified loyal

Christian Scientists "to organize immediately a Sunday School for the children." The notice continued with instructions for the lessons substantially the same as those which now constitute Article XX, Section 3, of the *Church Manual.* The Sunday School of The Mother Church *for children* was organized on October 5, 1895, having a Superintendent, an Assistant Superintendent, and two teachers. At first, the ages of the children were not limited. In January of the next year, the rule was adopted that children under twelve could be admitted, but children could not remain after becoming fifteen years of age.[1]

Another service for children occurred on Sunday, June 10, 1906, when The Mother Church dedicated its new edifice. On this day there were six services, at one of which—12.30 p.m.—children were given preference in seating the congregation; and they filled most of the seats. In its report of this dedication, the Boston *Herald* reported the children's service as follows: "It was 'children's day' at noon, for the service at half past twelve was specially reserved for them. They filled all the seats in the body of the church, and when it came to the singing, the little ones were not a whit behind their elders, their shrill trebles rising with the roll of the organ in almost perfect time. In every respect their service was the same as all the others."

---

[1] *Church Minutes*, Vol. II, p. 142.

The Mother Church, Administration Building, and Publishing House
prior to construction of the new Christian Science Center

The articles for children or young people which began to be marked as such in the *Christian Science Sentinel* about 1931 are not the first to be distinguished in such a way. From 1886 to 1889, *The Christian Science Journal* had a department headed "Home," which was mainly for children and parents. Then, except for an interval in 1889, it had a "Home and Children's Department" until 1891. For a few months in 1903, the *Sentinel* included a department or section headed "For the Children." The articles or items for children in the *Journal* from 1886 to 1891 consisted chiefly of healings by children, stories having a moral or spiritual point, poems, mostly reprinted, and reviews of books. Articles on Christian Science or on teaching Christian Science to children became more frequent toward the end of this period, but never became more than occasional. The section "For the Children" in the *Sentinel* contained articles and poems, partly reprinted, intended to interest and instruct juvenile readers; and it was a distinct improvement over the earlier departments in the *Journal*. From 1903 to 1931 articles on Christian Science for children or young people appeared in the *Sentinel* infrequently or occasionally and were not always headed as such.

For The Mother Church, reading from the Bible and the Christian Science textbook took the place of personal preaching in January, 1895, immediately after it occupied its first edifice. For branch churches, reading superseded personal preaching in April, 1895. At the annual meeting held in October, 1895, the Clerk's report included the following paragraphs: "Since we have occupied the church, the services have been attended by large congregations eager to listen [to] the words of Life, and on many occasions people have gone away, being unable to obtain seats.

"The sermons from our new Pastor, the Bible and Science and Health with Key to the Scriptures, ordained by our Pastor Emeritus, the Rev. Mary Baker Eddy, are doing incalculable good. Many cases have been reported of persons who, through years of invalidism had become tired of this life, have come to the services in despair, but through the power of the Spirit have been entirely healed of their infirmities, and have gone away praising God."

PART THREE
HISTORY

CHAPTER XXI

ITEMS FROM OUR LITERATURE

TO communicate what she had discovered and proved, Mrs. Eddy carefully chose the best means for doing this effectively and safely. For this purpose, she chose oral and written teaching, the oral to be based on the written. So, for one thing, Christian Science differs from other religions in the degree of its dependence on the Bible and on its own literature for communicating its doctrines to the public, for informing inquirers, and for instructing students.

As soon as Mrs. Eddy was prepared to impart her teaching, she composed and used a manuscript for this purpose entitled *The Science of Man, by Which the Sick are Healed.* Copyrighted in 1870, and first issued in handwriting, this manuscript was the beginning of Christian Science literature. It preceded the first edition of Mrs. Eddy's principal work, *Science and Health,* by five years. Printed editions of *The Science of Man,* differing slightly, were issued in 1876, 1879, and 1883. Afterward, Mrs. Eddy discontinued this pamphlet for separate use, but in 1881 she perpetuated its gist by putting its substance into her principal work, where it constitutes the chapter headed

"Recapitulation." In this textbook, now entitled *Science and Health with Key to the Scriptures*, parts of her first manuscript and pamphlet retain their original form. The following sentence is an instance (p. 485): "Not death, but the understanding of Life, makes man immortal."

The two sermons by Mrs. Eddy which are now published by themselves, *Christian Healing* and *The People's Idea of God. Its Effect on Health and Christianity*, were published as pamphlets in 1880 and 1883 respectively. The latter sermon, originally entitled *The People's God. Its Effect on Health and Christianity*, was also published in the second number of *The Christian Science Journal* (June 2, 1883). These pamphlets, therefore, are among the oldest parts of Christian Science literature. One of them was preceded by only *The Science of Man, by Which the Sick are Healed* (1870) and *Science and Health* (1875). The other was also preceded by the first number of *The Christian Science Journal* (April 14, 1883).

In the early history of Christian Science, other pamphlets by Mrs. Eddy, after having been discontinued as such, were partly copied into other works and became parts of her permanent writings. Thus, in 1885, she issued a pamphlet entitled *Defence of Christian Science*, the occasion for which was furnished by published attacks by two Boston ministers. The same defense was also printed in *The Christian Science Journal* for March, 1885. In 1887, this pamphlet was discontinued, but in the same year

Mrs. Eddy used much of its contents for the book now entitled *No and Yes,* which was first entitled *Christian Science: No and Yes.* In this book, extensive parts of the sections headed by questions (pp. 13–46) can be traced to the pamphlet *Defence of Christian Science.*

Since the books *Miscellaneous Writings* and *The First Church of Christ, Scientist, and Miscellany* consist of articles by Mrs. Eddy which had been published separately, more than a few of the articles have interesting histories by themselves. An instance is furnished by "One Cause and Effect" on pages 21–30 of the book first named. This article was originally published in the *Granite Monthly* of Concord, New Hampshire, for October, 1896. In that periodical, it was accompanied by an article headed "Rev. Mary Baker Eddy," by Septimus J. Hanna, which constituted a brief but excellent biography. The *Granite Monthly* containing these articles was sold by The Christian Science Publishing Society. Afterward, the publisher of the *Granite Monthly* printed the articles as a pamphlet called *Biography of and Essay by Mary Baker G. Eddy,* which had an extensive sale.

The article by Mrs. Eddy addressed "To the Christian World," which now composes pages 103–108 of *The First Church of Christ, Scientist, and Miscellany,* was first published in the *New York Sun* for December 16, 1898. It was reprinted in the *Concord* (New Hampshire) *Evening Monitor* of the next day. Then, after Mrs. Eddy had revised it, this article was published further in the *Independent Statesman* of Concord for December 22, 1898, in the *Christian Science Sentinel* for December 29, 1898, and in *The Christian Science Journal* for January, 1899. The occasion for this article was furnished by an English coroner's inquest, which accused two Christian Scientists of manslaughter because they did not heal a popular author, an American named Harold Frederic, who tried Christian Science for a short time during his last illness. He employed physicians before and after offering a brief opportunity to Christian Science. This inquest caused an international sensation; hence, Mrs. Eddy's appeal to all Christians commanded the attention of an immense number of readers at that time. Of course, it helped to stop the legal proceedings.

The Christian Science movement once had a periodical that did not last. From May 1, 1889, to April 15, 1891, The Christian Science Publishing Society issued a small semi-monthly periodical called the *Christian Science Series*. It consisted of twelve pages, containing four by seven inches of print, and had no cover. Advertisements of our literature always occupied a page or two, and one or two articles often occupied the remaining space. Sometimes there were several articles, and occasionally there was a poem. In the first five numbers and in two later numbers the articles were by Mrs. Eddy, and were reprinted from numbers of *The Christian Science Journal* which were earlier by several years. Thus, she furnished the articles for seven of the forty-nine issues of the *Series*. The articles for the other forty-two issues were diverted from the *Journal*, and were such as the *Journal* may have needed. In fact, it was chiefly the lack of enough important articles for both periodicals which required the *Series* to be stopped. The person chiefly responsible for the beginning of the *Series* was the Editor of the *Journal* at that time. Mrs. Eddy assented to the *Series* more than she approved of this undertaking. Most of the articles by Mrs. Eddy which were in the *Series* are to be found now in her *Miscellaneous Writings*.

The full name of the book commonly called *Miscellaneous Writings* includes the years 1883–1896. This contains most, but not all, of Mrs. Eddy's writings during this period which are not in her other books. Likewise, *The First Church of Christ, Scientist, and Miscellany*, could have had the years 1897–1910 as part of its name. This book contains most, but not all, of her writings during this period which are not in her other books. It contains only one earlier article. Mrs. Eddy chose the titles for both of these books, and she chose the entire contents for the first of them. For the second of them, she left a collection of articles which comprises most of its contents. There were reasons for concluding that she did not intend her selections for it to be exclusive. So, when the Trustees under Mrs. Eddy's will published *The First Church of Christ,*

Scientist, and Miscellany, they put into this book a few of her published articles which she had not selected for it.

From early in its history, the Christian Science movement has been aided by important pamphlets besides those which Mrs. Eddy wrote. *Writings and Genius of the Founder of Christian Science*, by Hanover P. Smith, was issued in 1886. This pamphlet, by a Christian Scientist who was closely associated with Mrs. Eddy in the Church of Christ, Scientist, and was a capable writer, must have helped to make her correctly known to the public. It was published by its author, but was advertised in *The Christian Science Journal*. *Christian Science and the Bible*, by the Rev. James H. Wiggin, was issued in 1886. He was the literary critic whom Mrs. Eddy had employed as is related in another chapter. Although issued anonymously by "Phare Pleigh," this pamphlet answered many clerical criticisms, and must have been enlightening to many readers. *Christian Science History*, by Septimus J. Hanna, was issued in 1899. Containing facts as to Mrs. Eddy's life and work, including her authorship of *Science and Health*, this pamphlet by a fully informed and experienced writer was circulated gratuitously, and must have been convincing to all fair-minded readers.

The *Christian Science Quarterly* has an interesting history; it can be traced to a beginning which was quite different from its present contents. In *The Christian Science Journal* from August of 1888 to March of 1889 there were "Bible Lessons" consisting of notes from the Christian Science standpoint on the International Sunday School Lessons used in Protestant churches. Other articles like them were in the *Journal* from August to November of 1889. All of these writings were from a single contributor, and they included comparatively few citations or quotations from Mrs. Eddy's writings. The Christian Science Publishing Society also issued these Bible Lessons as reprints from the *Journal*.

In January, 1890, the Publishing Society began to issue a monthly periodical called *The Christian Science Bible Lessons*. A committee appointed by Mrs. Eddy prepared its contents, the original members of which were Miss Julia S. Bartlett, William B. Johnson, Ira O. Knapp, and the Rev. Lanson P. Norcross. After three issues as a monthly, this periodical became a quarterly, and began to be spoken of as "the *Quarterly*," but its name was not changed formally until later. The Lessons in this periodical continued to be based on the International Lessons, but they were different from those which had been in the *Journal*. In particular, the new Bible Lessons were less like personal sermons; they consisted mainly of introductory comments and expository notes containing such information as might be found in reference works, parallel references to the Bible and, as the announcement read, "copious references" to the Christian Science textbook. For a time, the *Quarterly* included two Lessons for each Sunday; one like our present Lesson-Sermons; the other presenting citations to the Bible and *Science and Health* as explaining subjects or texts from the International Lessons. In The Mother Church, one Lesson was used for the Sunday morning service, the other was used for the afternoon or evening service, and either Lesson was used in the Sunday School. Therefore, it was by gradual development that our Lesson-Sermons ceased to have any connection with the International Lessons, and are now composed entirely of references to the Bible and our textbook as pertaining to our own subjects. Mrs. Eddy chose them, and she regarded them as having been given to her of God.

CHAPTER XXII

CENSURES NOW DISCREDITED

FOR a long time after Christ Jesus began to teach the Christian religion, the early Christians had to confront a persistent opposition based on fictitious reasons. Now, their experience has been and is being repeated in the experience of Christian Scientists. There were censures of Christian Science in its early history that are no longer heard or seen. This encouraging fact deserves to be better known. Furthermore, other canards or criticisms are completely discredited, and continue to be repeated only because ignorance is obdurate and hatred refuses to yield. Encouragement for Christian Scientists can be found even in instances of this sort. Then, too, the facts to be stated should be of interest to all fair-minded observers. Mary Baker Eddy discovered Christian Science in 1866, began to teach it in 1867, and issued her first book in 1875. Yet, this subject will be clearly and correctly known in the future immeasurably more than it has been in the past.

One of the first contentions against Christian Science denied its character as a religion. For this censure there was an excuse though not an actual reason. The Christianity then in vogue did not heal "all that were oppressed of the devil" (Acts 10:38). In particular, it did not "heal the sick" (Matthew 10:8; Luke 10:9). Hence, a new teaching that stressed healing the sick could be easily regarded as only another drugless cure until its actual character was communicated to the public. Furthermore, some of Mrs. Eddy's early names for her teaching did not necessarily denote that it was purely religious or spiritual. This comment applies to "Metaphysical Science" and "Moral Science," which terms she used at first more often than Christian Science. So the censure just stated began at an early date; and it continued until after Christian Science was represented by a Church and until after the Church of Christ, Scientist, became extensively known as a Christian denomination.

Among the next criticisms of Christian Science were that Christian Scientists did not accept the Bible and did not believe in God. Although these criticisms were not the same, they were closely related and had similar pretexts. Mrs. Eddy interpreted many passages in the Bible so as to give them new meanings. She also taught new concepts of God; and in doing this she used names for God that were partly new. On the other hand, few persons in all history, if anybody, have had more faith in the Bible and in God than she had, and her devout attitude toward the Bible and toward God was evident from the first of her teaching. It left no plausible reason for the canards or misstatements in question. Yet, they persisted for a surprising length of time. They continued until after Mrs. Eddy had refuted them explicitly in the Christian Science Tenets.

A criticism that followed the two criticisms just mentioned was that Christian Scientists did not believe in Christ. Although often expressed in these words and in other misleading terms, this contention was attached to the fact that Christian Scientists do not regard Jesus as God. Mrs. Eddy acknowledged that Jesus demonstrated the Christ. She accepted all that he said about himself, including his sayings to the effect that he was Christ but was not God. (See Matthew 19:17; Mark 10:18; Luke 18:19; John 4:24–26, 8:40.) Furthermore, she added to the common definitions of Christ in the most helpful way; she explained and proved the Christ to be ever available and ever present. Declining to be limited by merely personal concepts, she gave to this term a new meaning as follows: "Christ is the true idea voicing good, the divine message from God to men speaking to the human consciousness."[1] In I Corinthians 10:1–4, Paul had spoken of the Christ in an impersonal way, and Mrs. Eddy's explanation of the Christ as the impersonal Saviour is one of the most helpful developments in the history of religious thought.

Another censure like the foregoing contentions was that Christian Scientists did not believe in prayer. This canard was like the others here mentioned in having a

---

[1] *Science and Health*, p. 332.

similar pretext—mere differences between religionists—and in having been devised by clergymen or ministers. It was attached to the fact that Christian Scientists have a deeper and larger concept of prayer than was common among other religionists. In particular, Christian Science prayer is based on divine law and is not limited to petitions. In 1885, a minister attacked Mrs. Eddy as "prayerless." [1] And he was neither the first nor the last opponent to do this. But this attack has been discarded. For one reason, the common concepts of prayer have broadened. Thus, it is now concluded from the Bible that adoration, declaration, and thanksgiving are among "the main constituents of prayer." [2] Surely, some degree of credit can be given to the Discoverer of Christian Science because many people in diverse communions are gaining more enlightened concepts of God, Jesus, the Christ, and prayer.

Another of the first censures of Christian Science was that its cures were brought about by mesmerism. For this contention, also, there was an excuse though not an actual reason. Mesmerism was then a subject of public interest, and Mrs. Eddy had been a patient of a drugless physician, P. P. Quimby, who employed it. She had also praised him in newspapers before she learned to distinguish between mental methods. Hence, the assertion by either casual or critical observers that she taught and practiced mes-

---

[1] See *Miscellaneous Writings*, p. 133.
[2] *New Standard Bible Dictionary*, p. 724.

merism was not strange until she corrected it thoroughly. This she did as she found opportunities; but the censure in question was circulated by opponents of her work, and it persisted, in spite of all corrective efforts, until long after it had been refuted in every feasible way.

The assertion that Mrs. Eddy got any part of actual Christian Science from "Dr." Quimby is a different but connected matter. That censure has been dealt with thoroughly in Chapter VI of this book.

There is a need today for Christian Science to be clearly distinguished from all mental methods to which it is opposed or which do not fulfill its requirements. Some of these methods are derived from mesmerism, and are contrary to Christian Science for this reason. Others should be regarded as counterfeits or substitutes; they are objectionable as such. Other teachings or practices may be praiseworthy for their own character, but should not be accounted the same as Christian Science.

How can this Science be distinguished from other teachings or practices? Mrs. Eddy has said that *"by knowing the unreality of disease, sin, and death,* you demonstrate the allness of God. This difference wholly separates my system from all others."[1] Christian Science attributes to God all actual being, all true consciousness, everything that is real. God, good, is the Principle of man and of all that constitutes his environment. Any contrary

---

[1] *Unity of Good,* pp. 9, 10.

seeming is unreal. Christian Science differs from other teachings or practices by its scientific use of such divine and spiritual truths to avoid or destroy evil and to demonstrate the innumerable aspects of good as constituting the only reality. For the reason indicated by the foregoing quotation and statement, Christian character is essential to progress in learning and practicing this Science.

A more evident criterion may be needed by inquirers or observers, and one is furnished by certain facts. They are that Christian Science was discovered by Mary Baker Eddy; its standard statement is in her book, *Science and Health with Key to the Scriptures;* and anybody who is qualified to expound Christian Science should be a member of the church that Mrs. Eddy founded. The Mother Church, The First Church of Christ, Scientist, organized in September, 1892, in Boston, Massachusetts, together with its branches throughout the world, constitutes the Church of Christ, Scientist. In most situations, the foregoing facts will enable an inquirer or observer to form an intelligent judgment as to whether a speaker or writer is expressing genuine Christian Science.

From time to time, critics of Christian Science have asserted that Mrs. Eddy obtained part of it, especially particular words, from philosophic idealism. If this criticism were valid, it would be no more important than the trace of early Greek philosophy to be found in the New Testament. For instance, the word "Logos" in the original text of John 1:1, 14, was also used in some Greek philosophical systems, in which this term meant "the rational principle of the universe."[1]

In philosophy, "idealism" is defined as follows: "(a) Any theory which affirms that the universe is an embodiment of mind or that reality is essentially psychical;—called *metaphysical idealism*. (b) Any theory which identifies reality with perceptibility or denies the possibility of knowing aught save psychical reality;—called *epistemological idealism*."[2] Winston's definition is similar. It is to be observed that the foregoing definitions do not distinguish, as Christian Science does, between the divine Mind, including spiritual sense, and the counterfeit or opposite called mortal mind, including material sense.

Christian Science is both idealism and metaphysics, but not in any merely philosophic sense. It is not merely mental or psychic; it is divine and spiritual. In short, Christian Science presents a purely spiritual view of reality, including mental acts and states.

This point is elucidated by the following quotations from Mrs. Eddy's writings. "To grasp the reality and order of being in its Science, you must begin by reckoning God as the divine Principle of all that really is."[3] "The universe of God is spiritual,—even the ideal world whose

---

[1] *Webster's New International Dictionary, Winston Simplified Dictionary.*
[2] *Webster's New International Dictionary.*
[3] *Science and Health*, p. 275.

cause is the self-created Principle, with which its ideal or phenomenon must correspond in quality and quantity." [1]

For the present, scholastic science is limited to human concepts, but it admits the possibility of a higher mental power. "Science, we have now come to understand, cannot deal with ultimate reality; it can only draw a picture of nature as seen by the human mind. . . . Science must admit the psychological validity of religious experience. The mystical and direct apprehension of God is clearly to some men as real as their consciousness of personality or their perception of the external world. It is this sense of communion with the Divine, and the awe and worship which it evokes, that constitute religion—to most a vision seen only at moments of exaltation, but to the Saints an experience as normal, all-pervading and perpetual as the breath of life." [2] "The fact of the religious vision, and its history of persistent expansion, is our one ground for optimism." [3]

---

[1] *Miscellaneous Writings*, p. 217.
[2] *A History of Science and Its Relation with Philosophy and Religion*, 1929, by W. C. D. Dampier-Whetham, pp. 38, 485.
[3] *Science and the Modern World*, 1927, by A. N. Whitehead, p. 238.

CHAPTER XXIII

LEGAL AIDS AND HINDRANCES

THE first legal aid or hindrance experienced by the Christian Science movement may have been either an aid or a hindrance. In 1875, after Mrs. Eddy, then Mrs. Glover, had composed her principal work and had named it *The Science of Life*, she learned that another book had this title. In this situation, she changed the title of her book to *Science and Health*, while it was being printed, so that she could get a valid copyright. This incident is attested by a letter dated June 2, 1875, from Mrs. Eddy to the Copyright Office in Washington. That it may have been an aid, not a hindrance, is indicated by a paragraph in her Message to The Mother Church for 1902 (pp. 15–16).

In 1879 and 1881, Massachusetts statutes aided the Christian Science movement more than can be easily appreciated now, by enabling Mrs. Eddy and her followers to incorporate the Church of Christ, Scientist, and the Massachusetts Metaphysical College. These charters helped immediately to promote the new teaching, and later they served as precedents for the incorporation of additional churches and "institutes" for teaching Christian

Science, which also helped to give it a recognized standing in public estimation. Sometimes charters were refused. Even at Philadelphia in 1903, the final authority for the granting of charters refused one for First Church of Christ, Scientist, of Philadelphia. The officials gave different reasons at different times, but their last one was this: "Our laws recognize disease as a grim reality, to be met and grappled with as such." In short, the officials in so enlightened a community as Pennsylvania considered that they could and should limit the ideas to be taught as religion and Science.

A suit which Mrs. Eddy began in the United States Circuit Court at Boston, in 1883, was important then and is now, because the decree in that suit determined the issue whether she was the actual author of the pamphlet *The Science of Man* and the book *Science and Health*, which she had filed in the United States Copyright Office. The defendant was Edward J. Arens, formerly an avowed Christian Scientist, who had issued a pamphlet entitled *Christianity, or the Understanding of God as Applied to Healing the Sick*, consisting largely of statements copied from the pamphlet and the book just named. In his pamphlet Mr. Arens acknowledged indebtedness to P. P. Quimby of Belfast, Maine, and referred slightingly to "a work by Eddy." Thereupon, Mrs. Eddy brought a suit against him for infringing her copyrights. He defended it by alleging that Mr. Quimby, not Mrs. Eddy, was the actual author of the statements in question, and that she had taken them from manuscripts composed by him. This defense would have been sufficient if it could have been proved, but the defendant introduced no proof, and the court entered a decree for the plaintiff. After the decree had been entered, the defendant offered the excuse that the manuscripts by which his alleged defense could have been proved were in the possession of Mr. Quimby's son, who had refused to produce them as evidence in the suit. Such an excuse, however, is idle, for the production of evidence can be required by legal process. In these circumstances, the decree obtained by Mrs. Eddy against the Quimby canard should be conclusive with all fair-minded persons that she is the actual author of the Christian Science textbook.

In the early history of the Christian Science movement, there were many prosecutions against Christian Scientists for the alleged offense of practicing medicine without having a medical license. The first of these prosecutions was brought against Mrs. Lotte Post at McGregor, Iowa, in 1887. She was finally acquitted, after having been arrested, fined, and subjected to three trials. Witnesses called by the prosecution (indispensable witnesses) testified that her practice of Christian Science had healed them of cancer and tuberculosis. One of the last of such prosecutions was begun in New York City in 1911, and was decided finally by the New York Court of Appeals (People vs. Cole, 219 N. Y. Rep. 98). In this case, the highest court in New York State construed the New York medical law favorably to the practice of Christian Science, and Chief Judge Willard Bartlett expressed a further opinion which deserves to be regarded as historic. In a separate opinion he said, "I concur in Judge Chase's construction of the statute. But I would go further. I deny the power of the Legislature to make it a crime to treat disease by prayer." The United States Supreme Court has held that a statutory distinction between prayer or the practice of religion and other modes of drugless healing is reasonable and valid.[1] Very few legislatures, if any, have intended to forbid or restrict the practice of Christian Science, and many of them have either declined to do this or have enacted favorable provisions.

Christian Science practitioners have been subjected to even more serious trials. Thus, at San Bernardino, California, in 1893, Mrs. Eliza Ward was indicted and tried for manslaughter because she did not heal a patient who died. The prosecution was evidently instigated by ministers and physicians. Physicians gave testimony, based on a post-mortem examination, that an operation would have relieved the patient and would have prolonged his life. Until the Christian Scientist was called, the patient had been attended by a physician, who did not become a witness to explain why he did not perform the operation

---

[1] Crane vs. Johnson, 242 U. S. Rep. 339.

recommended retrospectively by the medical witnesses. Nor did the prosecutors have a tenable theory as to why a Christian Scientist, but not a physician, is liable to be punished as a criminal for failing to cure or heal. The trial by a judge and jury lasted five days, and resulted in a verdict for the defendant. The prosecution and verdict also gave an impetus to Christian Science in an extensive vicinity.

At Concord, New Hampshire, in 1907, a suit was begun which would be difficult to match for effrontery and injustice. It was brought by Mrs. Eddy's son, her adopted son, and three of her more distant relatives to have her adjudged incompetent to attend to her own affairs, and to have a receiver appointed with authority to hold her property, manage her affairs, and dispose of her estate as the court might decide to be prudent and wise. The circumstances indicated that certain publishers engaged in sensational journalism induced these plaintiffs to file such a suit as Mrs. Eddy's "next friends." Although Mrs. Eddy had put her property into the hands of prominent men as trustees, and she protested against the suit, the court entertained it, and appointed masters to hear evidence and report their conclusions. The masters began their hearing after the suit had lasted for nearly six months, and after Mrs. Eddy had asked for a speedy trial. Then the suit ended quickly. The masters called on Mrs. Eddy at her home, accompanied by two lawyers and a stenographer, and her part in this interview evidently left no possibility that the masters could make an adverse report. Thereupon, the plaintiffs withdrew the suit.

All of Mrs. Eddy's kin did not join in this abuse of legal process, and those who did had been deceived. Yet, two of the plaintiffs were Mrs. Eddy's son and adopted son, who had abundant reason to know that her eighty-six years had not impaired her mental vigor; hence, the suit in which they joined was for her an extremely trying experience. Even it, however, involved both aid and hindrance. For one thing, it disclosed the motives of the published attacks on Mrs. Eddy which had preceded the suit. Further, it furnished the occasions for interviews with Mrs. Eddy by persons whose opinions of her helped to form a just public opinion.

One of them was Dr. Allan McLane Hamilton of New York City, then the foremost American alienist, who called on Mrs. Eddy preparatory to becoming a witness. Afterward, in a statement given to the *New York Times* he said, "I found Mrs. Eddy seated in a comfortable armchair in her study, a large back room on the second floor of her house. She was simply attired in a dark dress and light sacque, relieved by a simple ornament, a diamond brooch. Her white hair was worn in the style made familiar by her pictures. Her face was thin, as was her body. I was immediately impressed with the extraordinary intelligence shown in her eyes. In aged persons the eyes are apt to appear dimmed, contracted, and lacking in expression. With Mrs. Eddy, however, they are large, dark, and at times almost luminous in appearance. As she talked to me, or answered my questions, the play of expression on her features evinced unusual intelligence, and was in strict keeping with what she said. Her whole bearing was dignified and reserved, in perfect accord with what one would expect in a woman of education and refinement. . . . For a woman of her age I do not hesitate to say that she is physically and mentally phenomenal." Dr. Hamilton also examined a large number of letters from Mrs. Eddy written in the course of her daily life, and pronounced them "the products of an unusually intelligent mind."

The most important litigation involving Christian Science interests occurred in 1919, when trustees of The Christian Science Publishing Society contested the power of the Directors of The Mother Church to supervise their work and to remove a trustee. Thus, these trustees attempted to separate the Publishing Society from The Mother Church. At the same time, a dismissed member of The Christian Science Board of Directors contested his removal from it. Thus, he attempted to divide the five Directors of The Mother Church into two boards, one under the deed from Mrs. Eddy to the original Directors, and one under the *Church Manual*. Happily for all mankind, both of these attempts were completely frustrated by decisions of the Supreme Judicial Court of Massachusetts. [1] In these cases, the court manifested both the ability to comprehend Mrs. Eddy's gradually developed plan for The Mother Church and the disposition to uphold it in all respects. In effect, these decisions fulfilled a prophecy once made by Mrs. Eddy to one of the members of her household, Miss Shannon, that the *Church Manual* "will be acknowledged as law by law."

As a whole, the experience of Christian Scientists in contact with human law can be said to confirm Mrs. Eddy's statement: "Justice is the moral signification of law. Injustice declares the absence of law." [2]

---

[1] Eustace vs. Dickey, 240 Mass. Rep. 55; Dittemore vs. Dickey, 249 Mass. Rep. 95.

[2] *Science and Health*, p. 391.

CHAPTER XXIV

AMONG THE EARLY WORKERS

ONE of the most helpful among the early Christian Scientists was Miss Julia S. Bartlett. Her service, also, continued for a long time. She was an active Christian Scientist for forty-four years—from 1880 to 1924, and was one of many who served the Cause of Christian Science with unswerving faithfulness and consecration during those years. Miss Bartlett became interested in Christian Science in April of 1880; she studied this subject with Mrs. Eddy in October of the same year; she began her active service at that time.

Julia S. Bartlett was born at East Windsor, Connecticut, in 1842. One of her father's ancestors came to America from England in 1632, and was one of the colonists who settled Hartford. Her mother's family name was Allen. Her father passed on when Julia was thirteen years old; her mother followed him three years later; which changes left her as the eldest of six children. The obligations that devolved upon a girl of sixteen as the eldest of six orphans not only advanced her maturity but also developed her motherly qualities.

The rearing given by Mr. and Mrs. Bartlett to their

children, so far as it went, was entirely wholesome. These parents also left to their children an estate large enough to support them in a moderate way. As a child Julia attended a public school. Later she had private teaching and attended an academy for a short time. Then she went to a boarding school for about three years. At all of these schools, but particularly at the boarding school, she attained a high standing for deportment and scholarship.

Miss Bartlett's approach to Christian Science was impelled by two factors. The religion that she accepted from "conversion" did not satisfy her longing for religious truth. Besides this, a long-continued lack of health culminated in years of suffering during which she was an invalid for whom several physicians promised no permanent relief. Then, at the age of thirty-eight years, while living in Connecticut, she heard of Christian Science from a friend who sent a circular describing the Church of Christ, Scientist. It had been founded in Boston during the preceding year, and used this means, among others, of making itself known to the public.

What interested Miss Bartlett particularly was the announcement in the circular in Mrs. Eddy's words, "This church is designed to perpetuate the teachings of Jesus, to reinstate primitive Christianity, and to restore its lost element of healing." [1] She saw no reason why the sick should not be healed now as they were by the primitive

---

[1] See *Church Manual*, p. 17.

Christians. So, she sent for the book, *Science and Health* by Mrs. Eddy, and asked her friend to ask Mrs. Eddy to recommend a practitioner. Mrs. Eddy recommended her husband, Asa G. Eddy, to Miss Bartlett, and the result of his work for her was a quick healing.

"My one desire above all others," Miss Bartlett wrote in her reminiscences for The Mother Church, "was to see and know the one through whom all this great good had come to the world and to be taught the truth by her, that I might help others." In about four months after she first heard of Christian Science, she applied to Mrs. Eddy for teaching, and was accepted. This interview, which occurred at Lynn in Mrs. Eddy's home, Miss Bartlett has described as follows: "I felt her love which always made her thoughtful for others, and was perfectly at ease in her presence. She was beautiful, but rather more slender at this time than at a later period. She made arrangements with me about entering her class, and as I knew she had much to attend to, I made my call short. What most impressed me at this first meeting was her spirituality and the place she occupied in the world. Yet she met me just where I was, so simply and sweetly, mindful even of the little things for my comfort. As I went from her presence, I was thinking of the days when I could go to that little home and listen to her wonderful teachings."

There were only two other pupils in the class when Miss Bartlett first studied with Mrs. Eddy. This class was held in Mrs. Eddy's home at Lynn before she opened the Massachusetts Metaphysical College. After the class, Miss Bartlett and another pupil lingered at Lynn and saw Mrs. Eddy several times. Alluding to these interviews or visits, Miss Bartlett wrote, "And her conversation when with us was always an inspiration and instructive."

At this time, Miss Bartlett also attended her first Christian Science Sunday service. It, too, was held in the parlor of Mrs. Eddy's home. "There were about twenty people present," Miss Bartlett wrote. "Mrs. Eddy preached the sermon, which healed a young woman sitting near me of an old chronic trouble which physicians were unable to heal. Her husband, who was present with her, went to Mrs. Eddy the next day to thank her for what had been done for his wife."

In 1881, Mrs Eddy called Miss Bartlett to Boston for Christian Science work. Accordingly, she and another of Mrs. Eddy's pupils, Mrs. Abbie K. Whiting, sought rooms for them to use together in this work, but they encountered many refusals to let rooms for this purpose. Finally, they obtained desirable rooms in Charlestown, which is now a part of Boston, but was then a suburb. They planned to hold meetings every Friday evening to explain Christian Science and to tell what it would do for people, but months of effort were required to get their first audience, consisting of eight curiosity seekers. Miss Bartlett and Mrs. Whiting even went from house to house speaking of

Christian Science and leaving a pamphlet containing the sermon *Christian Healing* by Mrs. Eddy.

Miss Bartlett and Mrs. Whiting made a success of their Charlestown mission. They also accepted other opportunities to help Mrs. Eddy to conduct and extend the Christian Science movement. Thus, in 1882, when she went to Washington for three months, she chose Miss Bartlett to "substitute for me." This quotation is from a letter to Miss Bartlett dated January 20, 1882, in which Mrs. Eddy continued as follows: "See that the Christian work of this church is preserved, and dear Mrs. Whiting will help you." When Mrs. Eddy returned from Washington in April of 1882, she invited them to leave their Charlestown mission—in which Miss Bartlett's practice had increased to about thirty patients a day—and live with Mrs. Eddy in Boston, where she had acquired a desirable house for her home and for the Massachusetts Metaphysical College. Both of them accepted this invitation, and Miss Bartlett continued in Mrs. Eddy's household for about two years, rendering helpful service as requested.

At this time, when Mrs. Eddy's age was from sixty-one to sixty-three years, she had, as Miss Bartlett has recorded, the delicate complexion of youth, often with pink color in her cheeks, her eyes had a wonderful expression, and her entire countenance was radiant with spiritual beauty. Mrs. Eddy appeared to be as busy as one could be, and her work accumulated constantly, but she accomplished more and more, and never appeared to be in haste. In 1883, when she began to edit and publish *The Christian Science Journal*, it seemed that she could not possibly do this additional work, but she did it. At this time she was Pastor of the Church of Christ, Scientist, President of the Christian Scientist Association, President of the Massachusetts Metaphysical College, and Leader of the Christian Science movement. Besides other duties in these capacities, she carried on a large correspondence and received many calls from inquirers and students.

Miss Bartlett witnessed many healings by Mrs. Eddy, and related a few of them in her reminiscences. Here are two that Miss Bartlett related:

A man who walked with crutches went to hear Mrs. Eddy preach in Hawthorne Hall. Two people, one on each side, helped him up the steps at the entrance. After the service, he left the hall carrying the crutches under one of his arms. Miss Bartlett saw this man enter and leave. [1]

A lady who was a physician had a chronic trouble of long standing and called on Mrs. Eddy to talk with her about it. Afterwards she called on Mrs. Eddy to tell her that she had been entirely free from the trouble since the first call. And she gave to Mrs. Eddy a diamond ring, an heirloom, as an evidence of her gratitude. Miss Bartlett was with Mrs. Eddy when this lady called the second time.

---

[1] *Mind in Nature*, June, 1885, p. 62.

About March 1, 1884, a physician having a patient at Littleton in northern New Hampshire whom he and other physicians had not been able to heal sent the patient to Miss Bartlett for Christian Science treatment. Nine days later the patient returned to the physician perfectly well. For his assurance, she remained in his home for two weeks before going on to her own home. When her neighbors learned what Christian Science had done for this sufferer, some of them arranged with a correspondent to ask Miss Bartlett to visit their town as a Christian Scientist. This she did for eleven days in April, 1884.

While staying with her first Littleton patient, Miss Bartlett delivered two addresses in a hall, and gave the rest of her time to receiving and treating patients. After the first day or two, they kept her busy until late at night, and most of them were healed. Part of these health seekers came from other towns. As she wrote to Mrs. Eddy from Littleton: "There is a perfect *rush* of patients. Three M. D.'s are sending me patients. . . . I am turning away ten or a dozen patients every day that I cannot find time to see. . . . I am just *thronged*." In after years, Miss Bartlett visited other places to do healing or healing and teaching, but this experience at Littleton continued to be most vivid in her thought.

In August of 1884, Miss Bartlett was a pupil in the first Normal class taught by Mrs. Eddy in the Massachusetts Metaphysical College. Consequently, Miss Bartlett herself became an authorized teacher of Christian Science. At first reluctant to assume the obligations of a teacher, she yielded to Mrs. Eddy's persuasion, and became one of the first of Mrs. Eddy's pupils to begin teaching. Miss Bartlett taught her first class in September of 1884, and taught her last class in 1922. Most of her teaching was done in Boston, but during the years 1886–1889 she taught classes at Littleton, New Hampshire (two classes); several places in Vermont; Atlanta, Georgia; Calais, Maine; Fredericton, New Brunswick (two classes); St. John, New Brunswick (two classes); Halifax, Nova Scotia; and Logansport, Indiana. During these years, she may have taught other classes at other places. All of this itinerant teaching was done before 1891, when Mrs. Eddy spoke against it. [1]

It is difficult to mention all of the positions filled and services rendered by Miss Bartlett, but they include those in the following list. For the Church of Christ, Scientist, she was its President for one year, its Treasurer for over five years, and one of its Directors for over six years. She also served on many of its committees. Thus, she was an original member of its Committee on Bible Lessons. For the Massachusetts Metaphysical College she was one of its constituent members as a corporation. For the National Christian Scientist Association, she was one of the Christian Scientists who formed it, she was a member of its Executive

---

[1] *Retrospection and Introspection* 82:9–16; 88:27.

Committee for one term, and she was its Treasurer twice. For The Mother Church, The First Church of Christ, Scientist, she was one of the original First Members, and she continued to be a First Member or Executive Member from 1892 until this office was abolished in 1908.

Miss Bartlett, the earliest of Mrs. Eddy's pupils to survive her, was a guest or helper in Mrs. Eddy's home more than a few times after living with her for two years. The last time Miss Bartlett saw Mrs. Eddy was only a short time before Mrs. Eddy passed on. The Mother Church has fifty-three letters from Mrs. Eddy to Miss Bartlett, including one dated October 29, 1880, written soon after Miss Bartlett first studied with Mrs. Eddy. The following quotation is from that letter: "Do not forget to be strong in the clear consciousness that you are able to heal and no counter mind can make you weak for a moment through fear or a lack of confidence in your power or rather understanding. Remember God, Truth, is the *healer*, the balm in Gilead, and our only Physician, and can never be insufficient for all things."

CHAPTER XXV

EARLY HISTORY OF CHRISTIAN SCIENCE IN THE BRITISH ISLES

IN 1908 Mrs. Eddy wrote, "Forty years ago I said to a student, 'I can introduce Christian Science in England more readily than I can in America.' "[1] Forty years before 1908 (1868) was near the beginning of the Christian Science movement. Evidently, she looked for the development of Christian Science in the British Isles long before it had a single adherent there. Her acts and letters show that she kept up a continuous interest in this subject. In 1888 and 1889 she considered going to London to teach a class or classes there. For one reason, a counterfeit teaching, involving misrepresentation of Mrs. Eddy, was hindering the introduction of genuine Christian Science. Presumably, she decided against going because she had much else to do and because her students could attend to the immediate need in the British Isles. That Mrs. Eddy continued to regard London favorably, not discouraged by persistent difficulties there, is shown by a letter dated April 15, 1899, in which she spoke of that city as "the most important field outside of the United States."

---

[1] See *Journal*, Vol. XXVI, pp. 297–298.

In the British Isles, Christian Science was an almost unknown subject until May 26, 1885, when *The Times* of London published a two-column letter from a Boston correspondent, with a column of editorial comments thereon. Headed "Mental Healing in Boston, U. S. A." the letter presented Christian Science as the largest division or section of mental healing, and presented it in a respectful way. Naming Mrs. Eddy as the Leader of the Christian Scientists, it distinguished them from other mental healers because, it stated, they have a theology which they regard as essential to their theory. As regards healing, the correspondent found an abundance of positive testimony from people, undoubtedly honest, who claimed to have been cured by Christian Science of organic disease of long standing, but he was difficult to convince; he was disposed to assume other explanations for such extraordinary recoveries. The following excerpt is from the above-mentioned letter: "Hawthorne Hall, where the Christian Scientists worship, is thronged for an hour before the time for service each Sunday. So eager are people to hear that after the standing room is all taken people crowd around outside the doors, where they can catch only an occasional word or two. The service consists of ordinary devotional exercises preceding a sermon by Mrs. Eddy."

The editors of *The Times* were disposed to scoff. They reviewed the Boston letter fairly, but they alluded to it as "entertaining," and they attributed the success achieved by Christian Science to the credulity of the Boston people. The following excerpts from the editorial illustrate its tone: "In these latter days the world refuses to be profoundly moved by the birth of a new faith. . . . Boston still retains a large share of the fresh receptiveness of an earlier age. . . . It is agitated to its centre by the appearance of a system which we find it hard to classify, since it is at once an art, a science, and a religion." Of course, the compatibility of religion and Science has become more evident everywhere since 1885. At that time, Mrs. Eddy's first book on Christian Science had been published only ten years, and the Church of Christ, Scientist, had been founded only six years.

The first residents of the British Isles to become Christian Scientists were Mr. Graves Colles and Mrs. Marjorie Colles of Killiney, near Dublin, Ireland. She was an Englishwoman; her father was an Anglican clergyman. Mr. and Mrs. Colles heard of Christian Science in 1887 from a friend in the United States. Impressed by what they heard, they sent for Mrs. Eddy's book, *Science and Health with Key to the Scriptures*. Benefited and further impressed by reading it, they went to Boston to learn more about Christian Science from Mrs. Eddy. They had several interviews with her, and arranged to be in one of her classes. Accordingly, they were in the class of the Massachusetts Metaphysical College that Mrs. Eddy taught in March, 1888, and were the first British subjects to get her teaching. Mr. Colles became an avowed Christian Scientist, but did not become so active as Mrs. Colles. She became an ardent worker. She was the first person in Ireland to be a member of The Mother Church, her membership dating from July 1, 1893, the first inhabitant of the British Isles to be a Christian Science practitioner, and the first to be an authorized teacher. She did little class teaching, but was consistently active as a practitioner. She began to practice soon after studying with Mrs. Eddy in March, 1888, but did not have a practitioner's card in *The Christian Science Journal* until December, 1893. Moving from Ireland to England—to Monmouthshire and to London—in the middle of the 1890's, she contributed financially as well as otherwise to the development of Christian Science in Great Britain. Mrs. Colles visited Mrs. Eddy at Concord, New Hampshire, in 1893 and 1897, and in 1898 she was in the last class that Mrs. Eddy taught.

The next residents of the British Isles to become Christian Scientists were Mr. Marcus Ward and Mrs. E. Blanche Ward of Belfast, Northern Ireland. She, too, was an Englishwoman. Mr. and Mrs. Ward became interested in Christian Science in 1889, while living for a few years in New York. They had class instruction from an authorized teacher there in 1890. Returning to Belfast in 1891, they endeavored to introduce Christian Science there, but continued efforts obtained few or no permanent results. In

1892, Mr. Ward having passed on, Mrs. Ward moved to Birkenhead, near Liverpool, where she tried the distribution of Christian Science literature. In 1893, she was in Boston for five months. While there, she studied with another authorized teacher, as was possible then, applied for membership in The Mother Church, and engaged in the practice of Christian Science. Later in the same year, she settled at Bedford, England, as a practitioner. She was one of the first three students of Christian Science in the British Isles to become a member of The Mother Church, her membership dating from September 30, 1893. She was also one of the first two inhabitants thereof to have a card in the *Journal*, she and Miss Catharine Verrall having such a card together in Boston from March to August, 1893. She was also the first person in England to have a card in the *Journal* from England, from Bedford in September, 1893. In 1894, gladdened by encouraging results at Bedford, she removed to London to continue her practice and to hold Christian Science services. From that time, she has had an active and prominent part in the development of Christian Science in the British Isles. In 1898, Mrs. Ward visited Mrs. Eddy at Concord, New Hampshire, and in 1899 she became an authorized teacher as a certified member of the first class in the newly organized Board of Education of The Mother Church.

The first person living in England to acquire a per-

manent interest in Christian Science was Miss Catharine
Verrall of Falmer, near Brighton. She heard of this subject in 1890, and the reading of *Science and Health* in
1891 made her interest permanent. Acquainted with Mrs.
Colles and Mrs. Ward, she was aided in her progress by
visits with them in 1891 and 1892. Referring to the first
of these visits, Miss Verrall has written, "The practical
proofs of Christian Science I saw in Mrs. Colles' house
would fill a book!" In 1893, Miss Verrall was in Boston
for five months, where she applied for membership in The
Mother Church, studied with an authorized teacher, and
engaged in the practice of Christian Science. She was the
first inhabitant of England to become a member of The
Mother Church, her membership dating from July 1,
1893. She was also one of the first two people in England
to have a card in the *Journal*, she and Mrs. Ward having
such a card as stated in the foregoing paragraph. After an
interval divided between England and New York, Miss
Verrall returned to England in 1895. Since then, she has
been an active Christian Scientist, in Brighton, in London,
and again in Brighton.

The first resident of Wales to acquire a permanent
interest in Christian Science was Miss Frances Williams
of Llangammarch Wells. Her father was rector of the
Church of England there, and she was its organist. She
heard of Christian Science in 1892 from a friend living
in New York. Getting a copy of *Science and Health* in

the same year, Miss Williams immediately became an earnest student thereof, and later had class instruction from an authorized teacher in London. As Llangammarch Wells was a health resort, she accepted favorable opportunities to speak of Christian Science to visitors there, but she felt obliged to limit her activities as a Christian Scientist because of her father's position. Miss Williams joined The Mother Church in 1915, and has been an active Christian Scientist for many years.

The first inhabitant of Scotland who acquired a permanent interest in Christian Science was Mrs. E. Rose Cochrane of Edinburgh. She was the first person living in Scotland to join The Mother Church, the first to have a practitioner's card in the *Journal*, and the first to become an authorized teacher. She became interested in Christian Science in or before 1892, through her mother, who lived in New York and had been healed by reading *Science and Health*. Mrs. Cochrane studied with an authorized teacher there in 1893. She joined The Mother Church on March 31, 1894, and she obtained a card in the *Journal* from Edinburgh in 1895. She was also a member of Mrs. Eddy's last class in 1898, thus becoming an authorized teacher. As a practitioner and as a teacher, Mrs. Cochrane had a prominent part in the early development of Christian Science in Scotland.

When Mrs. Colles studied with Mrs. Eddy in March, 1888, two other members of the class were Mrs. Hannah

Larminie of Chicago and Miss Anne Dodge of New York. Afterward, this coincidence had consequences in the British Isles, for each of them did Christian Science work there, and Mrs. Colles was instrumental in this regard. Mrs. Larminie had studied with Mrs. Eddy in 1885; she had done healing and teaching before she studied again in 1888. For a particular reason, she was willing to leave Chicago for a time. So Mrs. Colles' persuasion and Mrs. Eddy's approval induced her to visit Mrs. Colles for Christian Science work in Ireland. This Mrs. Larminie did from July to November, 1888. Then a chain of events and a letter from Mrs. Eddy extended her mission to London, where she stayed until the middle of 1889. At Dublin Mrs. Larminie did a considerable amount of healing and taught one class. In London she did more healing, and taught at least one class. Yet for reasons that included confusion caused by counterfeit teaching, only meager results from this seed sowing could be found after a few years. In a letter to Mrs. Eddy dated December 14, 1888, Mrs. Larminie wrote, "I am putting the dividing line between the false and the true, that the people may not be deceived." That this was her main purpose in London is also implied by Mrs. Eddy's letters to her at that time.

Miss Dodge was in London for Christian Science work from the summer of 1890 to the autumn of the next year, having Mrs. Eddy's approval for this mission. In a letter published in the *Journal* for October, 1890 (Vol. VIII, p.

301), Miss Dodge wrote, "Let Christian Science do healing work here, seen and acknowledged, and it is established for all time; consequently I shall devote myself to
healing, and do no teaching at all for the present—further
than to recommend the textbook to all." This plan she
followed during her stay in London. At first, she lodged
at 4 Atherstone Terrace. Later, she leased the house at
48 Stanhope Gardens, where she conducted services as
well as received inquiries and patients. Finally, she moved
to 10 Hanover Square, where she continued this method.
Miss Dodge had a practitioner's card in the *Journal* from
August, 1890, until after she returned to the United States
in the fall of 1891. Mrs. Colles helped her to conduct the
first services in October or November, 1890. She was also
with Miss Dodge for a month in February and March,
1891. In a letter to Mrs. Eddy dated February 27, 1891,
Miss Dodge said, "How I thank God that you have such
a student!" The services that Miss Dodge began in London were advertised in the *Journal* from February to
December, 1891, and were the first Christian Science
services announced in the *Journal* from the British Isles.
Then ensued an interval of four years having no public
services in London but not devoid of Christian Science
work.

The first Christian Science services in the British Isles,
to be held publicly and having a continuous history to
the present time, were held in one of the Portman Rooms,

First Church of Christ, Scientist, London, England

Baker and Dorset Streets, in London, in February of 1896. They were first advertised in the *Journal* under the heading of "Regular Sunday Services of Christian Scientists" in May of that year. The church's announcement in the *Journal* appeared first in the issue for September, 1897, and has continued to the present time. The original services in the Portman Rooms were conducted by Mrs. Ward as First Reader, aided by different persons who acted temporarily as Second Reader.

When the services just mentioned began in the first quarter of 1896, the only practitioners advertised in the *Journal* from the British Isles were Mrs. Cochrane at Edinburgh and Mrs. Ward in London. Mrs. Colles, who divided her time between London and Monmouthshire, and Miss Verrall, who had just moved from Brighton to London, were practitioners then, but were not advertised as such. Miss Verrall also served as librarian or bookseller in connection with the services in the Portman Rooms. Almost immediately afterward, another practitioner and another teacher from the United States, Mr. Albert G. King and Mrs. Julia Field-King—who were not related—arrived in London to engage in Christian Science work, and were advertised in the *Journal*. But the early history of Christian Science in the British Isles can be said to have ended before they arrived, that is, when the permanent public services, begun in London in 1896, were recognized by The Mother Church.

Other active Christian Scientists in the British Isles in or about 1896 included Lady Abinger, Mrs. Florence H. Boswell, Richmond I. Cochrane, Lord and Lady Dunmore, Miss Adrienne Eckford, Mrs. Sarah J. Winslow, and Miss Eleanor Winslow, and the following who later became teachers, Mrs. Hester Grant, Lady Victoria Murray, Miss C. Lilias Ramsay, Miss E. Mary Ramsay, Miss Violet Spiller, afterward the Honorable Mrs. Hay, and Mrs. Mabel S. Thomson. Of course this list may not include all who deserve to be mentioned. At that time, the entire number of Christian Scientists in the British Isles was small, but most of them made excellent records. They proved to be both steadfast and zealous.

Lady Victoria Murray had the great privilege of meeting Mrs. Eddy several times between 1898 and 1907. Alluding to these occasions, the former has described the latter in the following words: "Mrs. Eddy was always beautifully attired in some soft shade of grey or mauve satin. She presented a radiant picture with her white hair, bright, clear complexion, and eyes sometimes sparkling with gaiety, then suddenly transformed into luminous wells of Soul-filled thought. She showed interest and pleasure when my father [Lord Dunmore] talked to her of his travels, and of Scotland, and she expressed a desire to travel, especially that she might see the Holy Land. She clapped her hands and laughed merrily at his amusing stories, though it would not be long before she turned the conversation to spiritual subjects. . . . The harmony of Mrs. Eddy's voice was like music, flowing forth without exerted power or human will. Her strength was a deep calm. Her might, so tender and gentle, was the bright light of the majesty and meekness of self-oblivious love."

CHAPTER XXVI

EARLY HISTORY OF CHRISTIAN SCIENCE IN GERMANY

CHRISTIAN SCIENCE was discovered by Mary Baker Eddy in Massachusetts in 1866. She began to publish her writings on this subject there in 1875. Originally composed and published in English, they were not published in any other language for many years. The first translating of her writings that Mrs. Eddy authorized was from English into German; and from 1912 the authorized publication of her principal book, *Science and Health with Key to the Scriptures*, having alternate pages of English and German, gave a strong impetus to the Christian Science movement in Germany. Before this occurred, however, Christian Science had a goodly number of adherents there, after having several introductions that were distinct and separate.

The first German to become an avowed Christian Scientist was Hans Eckert of Cannstatt. Able to read and speak English, he began to study Christian Science in 1889, he had class instruction from an authorized teacher two or three years later, and he became a member of The Mother Church in 1893. During this time, he was in the

United States temporarily, at Los Angeles, California; Portland, Oregon; and Tacoma, Washington. In 1894, Herr Eckert returned to Germany. Soon he began to speak of Christian Science there, as he found opportunities, but the people in the vicinity of Cannstatt and Stuttgart evinced an interest in this subject slowly. After several years, most of those who had become interested in Christian Science joined in the holding of Sunday services in Stuttgart, for which he did the translating. In 1904, these informal services were succeeded by Christian Science Society of Stuttgart, a branch of The Mother Church having a card in *The Christian Science Journal*. Of this society he became the First Reader, and was named as such in the *Journal* according to the custom of that time. In 1913, this society was succeeded by First Church of Christ, Scientist, of Stuttgart, which has continued to the present time.

Christian Science had a more fruitful introduction into Germany at Hannover through Frau Bertha Günther-Peterson. She began to study this subject there in 1894, and became a member of The Mother Church in 1897. She, also, could read and speak English. Her father and her husband had been physicians, and she had assisted them in their professional work. Doing this had given her a great desire to help mankind cope with disease, and she had been reared in an atmosphere of sincere piety. She heard of Christian Science from a friend of German descent at Minneapolis, Minnesota, who had been healed by this Science after a physician had given her up to die.

In 1894, when Frau Günther-Peterson heard of this healing, she sent for a copy of the Christian Science textbook, *Science and Health with Key to the Scriptures,* and began to study it earnestly. After two years, she went to the United States for class instruction from an authorized teacher, and obtained this teaching at New York in November, 1896. In June, 1897, after visiting her friends at Minneapolis and doing some healing there, she returned to Hannover to make Christian Science known in Germany. Mrs. Eddy encouraged her in this undertaking by sending a loving message to her by her teacher. Frau Günther-Peterson announced herself as a practitioner at Hannover by a card in the *Journal* for October, 1897.

The first patient that Frau Günther-Peterson had after returning to Hannover was a dressmaker, Fräulein Isermann, who was afflicted with a dangerous disease, for which she had been advised to undergo an operation. Having heard that Frau Günther-Peterson had studied a new healing doctrine in America, Fräulein Isermann refused her consent to the operation until she had given the new teaching a trial. The result was that Christian Science completely healed her in three weeks. Then, her healing from the disease in question was discussed by her friends and the families for whom she worked. Soon, the reports of her healing and other healings spread beyond Hannover.

Consequently, within a year Frau Günther-Peterson had patients from eighteen different cities or towns; and the healings that they reported became known to many people in many districts of Germany.

In 1899, she became an authorized teacher of Christian Science by special permission from Mrs. Eddy, given because a Normal class for which she traveled from Hannover to Boston was postponed. In 1906, Frau Günther-Peterson received a teacher's certificate from the Board of Education of the Christian Science Mother Church, after having attended one of this Board's Normal classes. Many of her pupils became active workers, not only at Hannover, but also in other cities and towns in different parts of Germany and Switzerland.

In the summer of 1897, a few interested persons began to hold Christian Science services in Frau Günther-Peterson's home. For these services, she did the translating and acted as Reader. After a while, increased attendance called for more room; hence, a flat was rented in the same apartment house. After another while, a further increase in the attendance at these services caused the renting of a hall near the center of Hannover. In March, 1898, when the attendance was about fifteen, the Christian Scientists of Hannover organized as First Christian Science Church in Germany. One year later, it was reorganized as First Church of Christ, Scientist, of Hannover. At this time, the church had an audience of from three hundred to four hundred persons, but had only twelve members, because persons who withdrew from the "established" church were likely to encounter difficulties and incur detriments. Persecutions in the name of government had begun in the summer of 1898, and they continued intermittently for several years.

In February, 1900, Mrs. Eddy gave one thousand dollars to First Church of Christ, Scientist, of Hannover, for its building fund. The church bought ground in October, 1901, and dedicated the completed building in October, 1902. This building was the first one in Europe to be constructed for use by a Christian Science church. It was not, however, the first one in Europe to be acquired for this purpose. In 1897, First Church of Christ, Scientist, of London, bought and remodeled a building for its use. For this building, also, or for remodeling it, Mrs. Eddy contributed one thousand dollars.

Another distinct introduction of Christian Science into Germany occurred at Dresden through Mrs. Mary Beecher Longyear, of Marquette, Michigan, and Mrs. Frances Thurber Seal, of New York. While at Dresden during the winter of 1896–1897, Mrs. Longyear and another Christian Scientist endeavored to make Christian Science known there. Mrs. Longyear did some healing; and they gave three "informal talks" on Christian Science, which were attended by American, English, and German people. In *The Christian Science Journal* for June, 1897

First Church of Christ, Scientist, Hannover, Germany

(p. 142), Mrs. Longyear said, "In Dresden, there has been a wonderful awakening." When she returned to New York, she arranged with a teacher there to send one of her pupils, Mrs. Seal, to Dresden for Christian Science work, and Mrs. Longyear furnished financial support for this work there for several years.

In 1896, Christian Science healed Mrs. Seal of failing eyesight and threatened blindness. In November of that year, she studied this Science with an authorized teacher. Soon she began to practice healing; she also became evening librarian for one of its Reading Rooms in New York City. In December of 1897, she went to Dresden to begin Christian Science work there, even though she could not read or speak German. Her first patient there was a girl from Russia studying to be a singer; her second patient was the rector of the Episcopal church in Dresden. Both were healed quickly; and these healings led to others, and they to more—in Dresden, elsewhere in Germany, and in other countries.

Christian Science services began to be held in Dresden in January, 1898. At first, they were conducted only in English, but they began to be conducted in German in September of the same year. Mrs. Seal was announced as a practitioner at Dresden by a card in *The Christian Science Journal* for February, 1898. In the spring of that year, she opened a Christian Science Reading Room, using her sitting room in a boarding or lodging house for this purpose. First Church of Christ, Scientist, of Dresden, was organized in February, 1900. Before this, Mrs. Seal had moved to Berlin, and had been succeeded as a practitioner at Dresden by Miss Emily Cotton, whose card as such appeared in the *Journal* for November, 1899.

In January, 1899, Mrs. Seal became an authorized teacher, after having been admitted to the first Normal class of the Board of Education of The Mother Church. Not all members of this class were certified as teachers, but the Board gave a certificate to Mrs. Seal with the expectation that she would return to Germany and would make Berlin the center of her work. Accordingly, she moved from Dresden to Berlin in the autumn of 1899, after she had continued her practice at Dresden and had taught a class of five pupils there. This class included Miss Cotton, in whose house she had lived when she first went to Dresden. Afterward, Mrs. Seal held her classes in Berlin, but she often went to Dresden for the purpose of seeing patients and helping to carry on the movement there.

Christian Science has had a continuous history in Berlin from 1899. The indications are that Fräulein Johanna Bruno was the first German in Berlin to become a Christian Scientist. She was admitted to The Mother Church on June 3, 1899, after having studied with an authorized teacher in London. Able to read and speak both English and German, she did the translating for the first Christian

Science services in Berlin. She also began to practice healing there at about the same time. Her card as a practitioner appeared in *The Christian Science Journal* from June, 1900.

Mrs. Seal leased an apartment in Berlin in the summer of 1899, the owner agreeing that she could live in it and could hold meetings in it for the purpose of teaching Bible lessons. Christian Science services, open to the public, were held in this apartment from the first Sunday of October in 1899. They were first advertised in the *Journal* in December of that year. The first audience consisted of eight persons. The Readers were Mrs. Seal and Miss Amy Bentinck-Beach, both of whom came to Berlin from Dresden.

Mrs. Seal's first patient in Berlin was a concert singer, whose healing from several disorders, including blindness, became known widely. It attracted other patients, and led to many other healings. In a contemporary letter (from Berlin, April 30, 1900) Mrs. Seal wrote: "I have had all that I could do all winter. . . . I have had as many as thirty patients at one time; and had to have one of my Dresden students come and join me. She also is quite busy. Nearly all of the patients come from outside of Berlin, from all parts of Germany. . . . I have not had a dozen American or English patients since I came to Berlin, in October, and the majority speak no English."

In the *Christian Science Sentinel* for November 1,

1900, the clerk of First Church of Christ, Scientist, of Berlin, which had been organized in September, reported a lively and steadily growing interest in Christian Science among the Americans and the English in Berlin, but that most of the healing work had been done among the Germans. The number of practitioners had increased to four, who were busy and doing good work.

First Church of Christ, Scientist, of Berlin, was organized on September 20, 1900, by twelve members. From the first, the number of its attendants greatly exceeded the number of members. Many attendants were cautious about canceling other connections, and at least a few were deterred by the attitude of the police. Interference by the police began while the church was small, and continued intermittently for more than a year. Most of it consisted of notices or threats to landlords, which were intended to keep them from letting halls or apartments to the church or to its practitioners. In more than a few instances, leases actually were canceled or refused. Finally, however, the Christian Scientists obtained an admission from the head of the Berlin police that nothing they were doing was forbidden by German law.

In 1900 and following, the Christian Scientists in Germany had to accept or reject the suggestion that they should divide themselves from the Christian Science movement founded by Mrs. Eddy, and proceed separately. This argument presented itself particularly at Hannover and Berlin. In the end, however, all but a few of the avowed Christian Scientists in Germany either gave no regard to the suggested division or deliberately rejected it. All who are named in this chapter opposed division and maintained unity.

Frau Günther-Peterson, in 1899, and Mrs. Seal, in 1902, had the great privilege of an interview with Mrs. Eddy. On December 24, 1899, Mrs. Eddy received Frau Günther-Peterson at her home near Concord, New Hampshire. As Frau Günther-Peterson has written: "I was ushered into a little parlor at the left of the entrance. A few minutes later, our beloved Leader, then counting almost seventy-nine years, came down stairs with a light elastic step and greeted me with warm cordiality as 'dear child,' both of her outstretched hands taking mine. . . . Before leaving me she took me into her arms, kissed my forehead, and blessed me and my work." During this interview, as Frau Günther-Peterson has also written, Mrs. Eddy said, "I look upon the German nation as one of the chief supporters of Christian Science." For the reason that Christian Science had made little progress in Germany at that time, this statement by Mrs. Eddy was evidently prophetic.

Mrs. Seal went to Boston in June, 1902, to attend an Annual Meeting of The Mother Church. Incidentally, she went to Concord, where Mrs. Eddy resided. To Mrs. Seal's surprise, Mrs. Eddy called on her at her hotel. Mrs.

Eddy explained that she could not receive visitors then, and continued thus, as Mrs. Seal has written: "I could not let you go away without taking your dear hands in mine, and looking into your brave eyes, and saying Thank you; thank you for being brave and true, for facing error courageously and standing with Truth." This incident is one of many that illustrated Mrs. Eddy's acquaintance with the course of Christian Science affairs, as well as her appreciation of and interest in the accomplishments of her followers.

INDEX

INDEX

Index

Berlin, Germany, 248–251
Bible, the, 2, 46, 61; basis of Christian Science, 121, 151, 206; as impersonal Pastor (with *Science and Health*), 126, 134, 193, 194, 197; quoted, 52, 62, 64, 79, 85, 112, 134, 155, 206, 207, 211
Bible lessons *See* Christian Science Bible Lessons
Billings, Mrs. *See* Glover, Mary Baker (granddaughter)
Biographical Directory of Members of the American Congress, 33
Biography of and Essay by Mary Baker G. Eddy, 199
Birkenhead, England, 234
Blackman, Miss C. Lulu, 136, 137
Board of Directors *See* Christian Science Board of Directors
Board of Education *See* Christian Science Board of Education
Board of Lectureship *See* Christian Science Board of Lectureship
Board of Missionaries, 183
Bodwell, Miss Sarah J., 103
Boston, Mass., 19, 20, 25, 39, 78, 79, 83, 91, 95, 120, 124, 129, 137, 140, 142, 152, 174, 177, 228, 235; in 1840, 5; Mrs. Eddy's active ministry in, 67
Boston Herald, 192
Boston University, 67
Boswell, Mrs. Florence H., 240
Bouton, Nathaniel, 39, 53, 104
Bow, N. H., 4, 10–12, 17, 32, 35, 36
Bowdoin College, 28
Branch churches *See* Christian Science branch churches
Brighton, England, 235, 239
Brisbane, Arthur, 130, 131
British Isles, 100, 119, 177, 230–241
Brookins, Miss Mary, 141
Brooklyn, N. Y., 74
Brown, Rebecca (Mrs. Ira P.), 57, 58
Bruno, Fräulein Johanna, 248, 249

Brunswick, Me., 28
Bryan, Miss Jennie L., 139
Bubier, Samuel M., 57, 59
Burlington, Iowa, 22
By-Laws *See Manual of The Mother Church*

C

C. S. B. degree, 177
C. S. D. degree, 177
Calais, Me., 228
Calhoun, John C., 24
Canada, 120, 152, 174, 177, 228
Cannstatt, Germany, 242, 243
Carter, Mr., 66, 67
Catawba College, 28
Central Music Hall, Chicago, 73, 175
Charlestown, Mass., 224, 225
Chelsea, Mass., 76
Chestnut Hill (Mrs. Eddy's home), 98, 120, 131
Chicago, Ill., 73, 89, 124, 138, 167, 174–177, 237
Chicago Record-Herald, 130
Chickering Hall, Boston, 115, 165, 190
Children's services, 191, 192
Choate, Mrs. Clara E., 70
Christ, Mrs. Eddy's explanation, 207
Christening, 190, 191
Christian Healing, by Mrs. Eddy, 198, 225
Christian Science, based on Bible, 121, 151; confused with spiritualism and mesmerism, 69, 208, 209; counterfeits of, 230, 237; criticisms of, 67, 68; criticisms discredited, 205–212; differed from Quimby's teaching, 47–50, 52; discovery of, 43, 45, 54–56, 62–68, 148, 242; distinguished from other teachings, 111, 209–212, 231; early appraisals, 51, 109; early names, 206; early published statement, 110, 111, 150;

[256]

Index

Index

Church Manual *See Manual of The Mother Church*

Church of Christ, Scientist (organized 1879), 20, 114, 150, 153, 160, 161, 164, 166, 167, 170, 180, 181, 206, 213, 228, 232; abandoned charter (1889), 154, 170; close relation with Christian Scientist Association, 164; defined, 210; Directors of, 125, 154; early circular, 222; free dispensaries, 181, 182; government of, 185; informal organization (1889–1892), 170; Pastor, 187, 188, 226; Sunday School, 183, 189, 190; Sunday services, 161, 165, 183, 186, 189, 224, 231

See also Mother Church, The

Clark, Mr., 50

Clark, Mrs. Jane T., 50

Clark, Jonas B., 56

Class instruction, 134, 138–140, 168, 233, 236, 242, 244

See also Christian Science teachers; Eddy, Mary Baker, as teacher; Massachusetts Metaphysical College

Cleveland, Ohio, 93, 174, 176, 183

Cochrane, Mrs. E. Rose, 236, 239

Cochrane, Richmond I., 240

Collections, church, 188, 189

Colles, Graves, 232, 233

Colles, Mrs. Marjorie, 232–239

Colman, Erwin L., 84

Colman, Mrs. Janet T., 84

Columbian University (George Washington University), 32

Committee on Bible Lessons, 228

Committee on Publication, 120, 165

Communion Season, 132

Concord, N. H., 1, 3–5, 11, 12, 19, 22, 35, 51, 74, 75, 92–98, 104, 119, 121, 124, 125, 135, 157, 199, 217, 233, 234, 251

Concord (N. H.) *Evening Monitor,* 199

Congregational churches, 11, 12, 14, 39, 55, 133

Connecticut Odd Fellow, 105

Corser, Enoch, 37, 39, 104

Corser, S. B. G., 104

Cosmopolitan Magazine, 130

Cotton, Miss Emily, 248

Council Bluffs, Iowa, 116

Counterfeit teaching, 230, 237

Crofut, William Elmer, 93–95

Crosby, Miss Mary H., 83, 84

Curtice, Corban, 39

Curtis, William E., 130, 131

Cushing, Alvin M., 56–60

D

Dartmouth College, 7, 17–20, 22, 32, 33, 39

Dayton, Miss Mary Alice, 140, 141

Deadwood, S. D., 70, 71

Deed of trust, 156, 219

Deerfield, N. H., 28

Defence of Christian Science, by Mrs. Eddy, 198, 199

Democratic National Convention, 24

Democratic State Central Committee, 24

Denver, Col., 116

Detroit, Mich., 137

Dispensaries, 173, 180–183 *See also* Christian Science Reading Rooms

Division and Reunion, 1829–1889, by Woodrow Wilson, 5

Doctrine of the Will applied to Moral Agency and Responsibility, by Tappan, 16

Dodge, Miss Anne, 116, 117, 237, 238

Dodge, Grenville M., 116

Dover, N. H., 3

Dresden, Germany, 246–249

[258]

Index

Dresser, Mrs. Annetta G., 48, 49
Dublin, Ireland, 232, 237
Dunmore, Lord and Lady, 240

E

East Stoughton, Mass., 149
East Windsor, Conn., 221
Eckert, Hans, 242, 243
Eckford, Miss Adrienne, 240
Eddy, Asa G., 58, 88, 189, 223
Eddy, Mary Baker, acknowledged
debt to clergy, 39, 40
addressed National Christian Scientist Association 174–176
as Discoverer, 35, 45, 64, 68, 81, 84, 85, 102, 147, 149, 151, 153, 186, 205, 210; acknowledged, 167; early steps, 148; first glimpse, 54–61
as Founder, 35, 64, 68, 85, 125–127, 132, 150, 153, 166, 186; acknowledged, 167; established Christian Scientist Association, 162, 163; established Committee on Publication, 165; established free dispensaries, 181, 182; established impersonal Pastor, 126; established *The Monitor*, 131; established the National Christian Scientist Association, 172–176; established the periodicals, 126, 127; established Reading Rooms, 165; planned the organization of The Mother Church, 153, 154, 156, 220; wrote the *Manual*, 185, 186
as healer and practitioner, 58, 64, 69, 78–87, 122, 149–152, 160; acknowledged, 65, 67, 71; cases: anemia, 116, 117; asthma and heart disease, 74, 75; blindness, 72; brain fever, 71, 82, 83; childbirth, 84; consumption, 79; cripples, 66, 67, 76, 78–80, 226; crossed eyes, 70, 71; deafness and dumbness, 83; diph-

theria, 70; enteritis, 65, 81; hereditary heart disease, 72, 73; hernia, 73; inflammatory rheumatism, 65, 66; inherited lung trouble and an acute disorder, 75, 76; insanity, 81, 82; lameness, 74; a loathsome disease, 85; raises dead and dying, 79–81, 85, 86; shortened limbs, 66, 67; stomach ailment, 83, 84; tuberculosis, 73
factors in success, 77; instantaneous results, 67, 70, 121, 166; never chief occupation, 64, 85; through preaching, 74, 224, 226; through teaching, 73; unacknowledged, 65
as Leader, 85, 123, 125, 147–159, 226, 231; acknowledged, 35, 40, 95, 152, 167; addressed followers at Pleasant View, 96, 97; care over her Church, 119, 158, 159; clarified differences between Christian Science and so-called mental cures, 144, 168; depended on divine guidance, 147, 148, 159; instituted class instruction, 168; voluminous correspondence, 158, 219, 226
as lecturer, before discovery, 45, 105, 133, 147; on Christian Science, 89, 124, 152, 164, 187
as Pastor, 187, 188, 190, 191, 194, 226
as preacher, 65, 66, 73, 74, 79, 97, 114, 115, 120, 121, 152, 187, 198, 224, 231, described, 115
as teacher before discovery, 41, 42, 133
as teacher of Christian Science, 68, 72, 73, 84, 133–144, 149, 151, 157, 160, 167, 175, 197, 205, 221, 223, 232, 237; in classes, 73, 84, 114–117, 133, 134, 157, 223, 224; forbade note-taking, 135, 137; last

Index

EDDY, MARY BAKER, as teacher of
Christian Science in classes (cont.)
class, 99, 120, 127, 135, 141–143,
157, 233, 236; normal classes,
168, 227; required good health,
73
description of, 115–119; instruction on practice, 132, 166;
methods, 133, 134, 139, 140;
tribute to, 133
as writer before discovery, 40, 41,
45, 55, 102, 103, 105, 106, 133
as writer after discovery, 68, 86,
87, 89, 102, 104, 105, 107, 109,
125, 144, 148–150, 169, 199, 211,
212; autobiography, 125, 148;
first public statment on Christian Science, 110, 111, 150; literary style, 102, 108–112; pamphlets, 197–201; *Science and
Health*, 63, 103, 106–109, 125,
150–152, 166, 186, 213, 215; *The
Science of Man*, 63, 150, 197,
198, 205, 214; translations, 242
attacks on, 198, 208 *See also* "Next
Friends" suit
Bible and, 46, 51; interpretations
of, 42, 103, 140, 142, 206
biographical data, 1, 4, 158; early
years, 35–42; marriages, 36, 41–
46, 149
biographies, 57, 103, 199
chose title of Christian Scientist,
166
christened children, 190, 191
defection of a few early students,
129
descriptions of, 37, 38, 42, 69, 70,
88–101, 107, 114–123, 135–144,
151, 218, 219, 223, 225, 240, 241,
251
early interest in religion, 40, 41,
51, 53, 55
education, 1, 19, 20, 22, 36, 37, 103,
104, 147

family and early home, 10–16, 19–
27, 40, 41, 45, 46, 51, 102, 149
financial resources, meager, 41,
42, 46, 151
frailty, early, 19, 21, 22, 36, 39–49
passim
grandchildren, 70, 71, 191
grants of money to early churches,
246
healing, first marvelous, 54–63, 148
homes, in Boston, 71, 72, 78, 82,
83, 89, 124, 151, 162; at Chestnut Hill, 98, 107, 158; on Columbus Ave., 79, 225; on Commonwealth Ave., 66, 67, 90
in Concord, N. H., 67, 157; at
Pleasant View, 96, 97, 107, 251
in Lynn, Mass., 54, 56, 67, 69,
78, 80–82, 88, 150, 224
in Swampscott, Mass., 54, 57, 58
various early, 43–45, 56, 64, 76,
90, 131, 149
household, 120, 225, 229
interest in British Christian Scientists, 230; in German Christian
Scientists, 251
interviews with followers, 90, 99–
101, 119–123, 137, 138, 143, 223,
224, 232, 240, 251; by Dr. Hamilton, 218, 219; by newspapermen,
93–95, 130, 131
kinsmen, 28–34
letters, early, 38–41; from her
mother, 3, 16; from students,
237, 238; to students, 127, 131,
148, 170, 178, 225, 229, 237
life purpose, 151
love for children, 79, 191–193
marriage to Eddy, 45; to Patterson,
36, 41–46, 149
misrepresented, 230
opposition to, 124, 149; lawsuits,
30, 128, 129, 217, 218
portraits, 121, 122
prophecy about *Sentinel*, 127

Index

Index

Glick, Mrs. Jeannette, 74, 75
Glover, George Washington (husband), 3
Glover, George Washington (son), 36, 42–45, 70, 71, 217, 218
Glover, Mary Baker *See* Eddy, Mary Baker
Glover, Mary Baker (granddaughter), 70, 71
Godey's Lady's Book, 105
Granite Monthly, 199
Grant, Mrs. Hester, 240
Great Britain *See* British Isles
Green, Mr. and Mrs. C. E. L., 82, 83
Green, Josephine, 82, 83
Greene, Mr. and Mrs. Eugene H., 73
Grimes, James W., 22
Günther-Peterson, Frau Bertha, 243–245, 251

H

Halifax, Nova Scotia, 228
Hamilton, Allan McLane, 218, 219
Hanna, Septimus J., 127, 141, 199, 202
Hanna, Mrs. Septimus J., 141
Hannover, Germany, 243–246, 250, 251
Hanover, N. H., 7, 17
Hawthorne Hall, Boston, 65, 66, 226, 231
Hay, Hon. Violet S., 240
Hergenroeder, Miss Emilie, 121, 122
Hill, Miss Mabel, 92, 93
Hill's Daily Patriot, 26
Hillsborough, N. H., 11, 19, 20, 22, 24
Hillsborough Academy, 17
Historical Sketch of Christian Science Mind-Healing, by Mrs. Eddy, 169
Historical Sketch of Metaphysical Healing, by Mrs. Eddy, 169
Hodgson, Adam, 8
Holland, 100

Holmes, Augusta, 38
Homeopathy, 43, 46, 52, 59, 60
Hopkinton Academy, 32
Hotel Boylston, Boston, 165
Hotel Touraine, Boston, 165
Houston, Texas, 29
Howard University, 33
Hulin, Mrs. Emilie B., 74
Huntsville, Texas, 30
Hydropathy, 45, 46

I

I.O.O.F. Covenant, 105
Ilkley, England, 97
In Quest of the Perfect Book, by Orcutt, 106
Independent Statesman, 200
International Sunday School Lessons, 203, 204
Ireland, 232, 233, 237
Irwin, Frank E., 96
Isermann, Fräulein, 244

J

Jackson, Andrew, 13
Jefferson, Thomas, 13
Jesus, 52, 61, 73, 79, 95, 112, 127, 128, 134, 140, 144, 155, 167, 205, 207, 208, 222
Johnson, William B., 203
Jones, J. Henry, 88, 89
Journal of Christian Science, 187
   See also Christian Science Journal, The

K

Killeny, Ireland, 232
Kimball, Edward A., 108, 109, 138, 178
Kimball, Mrs. Edward A., 138, 139
King, Albert G., 239

[262]

Index

Index

Minneapolis, Minn., 75, 141, 244

Miscellaneous Writings, by Mrs. Eddy, 47, 54, 59, 60, 134, 140, 150, 175, 176, 188, 199, 201

Missionaries, 183, 184

Monroe, James, 13

Montreal, Canada, 120

Moral Science, 110, 150, 206

Mother Church, The, 117, 120, 122, 123, 132, 141, 170, 220, 229, 242, 243; Communion season abolished, 132; deed of trust, 156, 219; democratic character, 155, 156; Executive Members, 132, 186, 229; Extension dedicated, 192; First Members, 156, 171, 184–186, 229; founded, 125; missionaries, 183, 184; organization of, 138, 154, 171, 185, 210; original edifice, 91, 95; a permanent institution, 123; sermons in, 126, 193, 194; Sunday School, 190, 192, 204

See also Church of Christ, Scientist; *Manual of The Mother Church*

Murray, Lady Victoria, 240

N

Nahant, Mass., 39

Nashua, N. H., 3, 5

National Christian Scientist Association, 73, 153, 154, 170, 172–176, 179–181, 228; constitution (1886), 172, 173; Mrs. Eddy's address to, 73, 174–176

National Council of Women, 35

New England and New Englanders, 1, 4–10, 12, 36, 152

New England Conservatory of Music, Boston, 83

New Hampshire, 10–12, 18, 19, 22–25, 32, 39, 44, 149; in 1840, 1–9

New Hampshire Conference Seminary, 42, 133

New Hampshire Constitutional Convention, 33

New Hampshire House of Representatives, 24–27, 32

New Hampshire National Guard, 32

New Hampshire Patriot, 4

New Hampshire Patriot and State Gazette, 15, 24, 26, 105

New Hampshire Society of the Sons of the American Revolution, 33

New Hampshire Statesman, 26

New Hampshire Supreme Court, 23

New Hampshire Women, 103

New York, N. Y., 72, 116, 120, 124, 174, 176, 177, 183, 191, 215, 218, 233, 235–237, 244, 246, 247

New York Court of Appeals, 215, 216

New York *Evening Journal*, 130

New York Sun, 199

New York Times, 218, 219

New York University, 16

Newbury, Vt., 38

Newhall, Armenius C., 55, 56

Newhall, Mrs. Elvira, 88

Newhall, George, 55–57, 59

Newspapers, interviews with Mrs. Eddy, 93–95, 130, 131

Newton, N. C., 28

"Next Friends" suit, 30, 217, 218

Ninety-First Psalm, 74, 120

Nixon, Mrs. Helen Andrews, 90

Nixon, Paul, 90

No and Yes, by Mrs. Eddy, 169, 199

Norcross, Lanson P., 203

Normal classes, 138, 141, 168, 227, 245, 248

See also Class instruction

North Carolina, University of, 29

North Groton, N. H., 44, 45

Northfield, N. H., 11

Noyes, Mrs. Caroline D., 89

Index

Index

S

Sabbath, observance of, 12
St. John, New Brunswick, 228
Sam Houston State Teachers College, 30
San Bernardino, Calif., 216
Sanborn, Dyer H., 103
Sanborn, Mahala, 3
Sanborn's Grammar, 103
Sanbornton Academy, 4, 11, 20, 22, 32, 36, 37, 103
Sanbornton Bridge, N. H., 4, 5, 10–13, 22, 36, 37, 39, 41, 42, 65, 104
San Francisco fire, 188
Sawyer, Jennie E., (Mrs. Silas J.), 135, 136
Schools, 4, 6, 7, 28–30, 32, 36
    See also Academies
Science and Health with Key to the Scriptures, by Mrs. Eddy, 90, 111, 121, 122, 186, 223, 232, 235, 244; appraised, 51; copyright, 213, 214; first edition, 63, 64, 108, 148, 150, 197, 198; healings through, 236; impersonal Pastor (with Bible), 126, 193, 194, 203; index to, 106; marginal headings, 106; quoted, 62, 67, 148; "Recapitulation," 118, 198; revisions, 103, 106–109, 125, 148; studied by Mrs. Eddy, 113; textbook of Christian Science, 134, 210; translated, 242
"Sciences and the Senses," by Mrs. Eddy, 73, 74, 175
Science of Life, The, 213
Science of Man, The, by Mrs. Eddy, 63, 150, 197, 198, 205, 214, 232
Scotland, 177, 236 *See also* British Isles
Scott, John, 81
Seal, Mrs. Frances Thurber, 246–252
Sermons, impersonal, 126
Shannon, Miss, 220

Shelbyville, Tenn., 29
Shipman, Miss Emma C., 142, 143
Slavery question, 13, 14, 24, 26, 147
Smith, Clifford P., 122, 123
Smith, Hanover P., 83, 202
Smith, Hildreth H., (cousin), 28–31
Society for the Reformation of Morals, 4
South Carolina, 24
Spiller, Miss Violet (Hon. Mrs. Hay), 240
Spiritualism, 69
State Normal School, Huntsville, Texas, 30
Steinert Hall, Boston, 138
Steinway Hall, New York City, 124
Story of Religion as Told in the Lives of Its Leaders, The, by Potter, 104
Stoughton, Mass., 149
Students Christian Scientist Associations, 173, 176, 180
Stuttgart, Germany, 243
Sunday evening meetings, 182, 183
Sunday School, 183, 189–192, 204
Swampscott, Mass., 54, 55, 57, 58
Syracuse, N. Y., 117
Syracuse Post (Syracuse Post-Standard), 93

T

Tacoma, Wash., 243
Tappan, Henry Philip, 16
Taunton, Mass., 149
Teachers of Christian Science
    See Christian Science teachers
Temperance Society, 55
Ten Commandments, 62, 142
Thompson, Miss Abigail Dyer, 75, 76
Thompson, Mrs. Emma A., 49
Thomson, Mrs. Mabel S., 240
Thursday evening meetings, 187

Index

Tilton family, 41, 42, 45 *See also* Baker, Abigail B.
Tilton, N. H., 4, 14, 104, 149
Times, The (London), 231
"To the Christian World," by Mrs. Eddy, 199, 200
Tomlinson, Irving C., 120, 121
Toms, Mrs. Mary Henderson, 96, 97
Townsend, Luther T., 67, 68
Travers, Mrs. Eva Rogers, 90, 91
Tremont Temple, Boston, 174
Trustees under the Will of Mary Baker Eddy, 201
Twain, Mark (Samuel L. Clemens), 108, 109

U

Union Church of Christ, Bow, N. H., 12
United Fraternity, 18
United States Circuit Court, 214
United States Congress, 33
United States Copyright Office, 214
United States Supreme Court, 216
Unity of Good, by Mrs. Eddy, 169
Unity of Good and Unreality of Evil, by Mrs. Eddy, 169
University Press, 106

V

Vermont, 228
Verrall, Miss Catharine, 234, 235, 239

W

Wales, 235, 236 *See also* British Isles
Ward, Mrs. E. Blanche, 119, 120, 233–235, 239
Ward, Mrs. Eliza, 216, 217
Ward, Marcus, 233, 234
Washington, D. C., 22, 23, 32, 33, 116, 225
"Way-side Thoughts," by Mrs. Eddy, 106
Wednesday evening meetings, 126, 182, 183, 188, 189
Weeks, Mrs. Martha Philbrick, 42
Wheeler, Mrs. May, 56
White Mountains, 5, 38, 41, 44
Whiting, Mrs. Abbie K., 224, 225
Wiggin, James Henry, 106, 202
Wilbur, Sibyl, 57, 59, 60
Williams, Miss Frances, 235, 236
Wilson, Solomon, 20, 21
Wilson, Woodrow, 5
Winslow, Mrs., 58
Winslow, Miss Eleanor, 240
Winslow, Mrs. Sarah J., 240
Wool, Mrs. Alice Swasey, 69, 70
Writings and Genius of the Founder of Christian Science, by H. P. Smith, 202

Y

Yale University, 39